PRAISE FOR
I AM SILENT NO MORE

Lynz Piper-Loomis never wore a military uniform, yet she was thrown into battle. After years of loss and torture, she won the war, and then became a soldier—a soldier for country and for Christ. I am Silent No More is a must-read for everyone. No matter what you've been through, the events of Lynz's gripping and compelling real-life story are encouraging, and they ever-the-more prove Matthew 19:26 true: "With God, all things are possible!"
~ GENERAL MICHAEL FLYNN

Orphaned, abandoned, and rejected as a child, Lynz Piper-Loomis's incredible story will leave a lasting impression. Through faith and trust in God, she survived it all. Her testimony confirms that anyone can rise from the ashes after being thrown into a "life-fire" they never started.
~ Arizona Representative MARK FINCHEM

From beginning to end, a moving and powerful page turner chronicling the life of a woman whose world was turned upside down and inside out when she was much too young. Lynz Piper-Loomis is due a standing ovation for her determination and will to overcome!
~ MARY FLYNN O'NEILL

LYNZ
PIPER-LOOMIS

I am
SILENT
No
MORE

LYNZ
PIPER-LOOMIS

DEDICATION

I dedicate this book first and foremost to my Papa, my Heavenly Father. You, oh Lord, have been with me through each moment, and it is You that I give all gratitude, glory, honor, and praise. Thank You for raising me, nurturing me, loving me, and teaching me in Your ways. You are my life-line, my sole inspiration, and the beat of my heart. I pray that my heart will reflect You and beat to the rhythm of Your heart. You, Daddy, are the full satisfaction in my heart.

I also dedicate this book to my husband and my two girls. Their unwavering support and strength throughout this journey has been a blessing. My hope for my two girls is that they will be greater than me or what I could ever think or imagine. I know the legacy of my girls will be recorded in history as two women that had hearts after God's own heart. To my love, I cannot imagine this life without your love in it. You are the definition of a "brave heart". Your tenacity and perseverance in life encourages us all to dream the impossible dream and to never give up. Thank you for co-laboring in life together with me. Thank you for your sacrifice to this country and for our family. You are a rare gem, and I am excited to be in the next leg of this journey of life together.

I also dedicate this book to my mama—the great woman whose time was cut short, but a woman I learned so much from through her writings and quotes that lined her Bible and journals along with stories from her beloved friends. A great woman who taught me to walk in the fear of the Lord at a young age, and to walk unashamedly, fearlessly belonging only to God. A mother who laid her life down daily for me and for others, and a woman who taught me what it really means to live like Christ. The greatest testimony to her life was the lives of those she touched and testified after her arrival into the throne room of Heaven. I am thankful for the "no's" my mother said in life in order that she could say "yes" to God and for me. Her roots ran deep into the wells of the Lord, and that is truly one of the greatest legacies one may leave for us. I am thankful for the revival fire she carried in heart for others and her yearning after the things of God daily. For now, I cherish her beautiful legacy.

There were two particular families who were dear friends of mine growing up, and my Momma's closest friends. I want to thank you for being there when I tried to commit suicide, when I was broken, and when I thought I had nowhere to turn to. Thank you for holding me fervently in prayer when I was cut off from you for those years of hell. You blessed my dear mother with your sisterhood friendship, and God has used you in mighty ways beyond what you could ever fathom. I am eternally thankful to Papa in Heaven for each of you and your families. Thank you for never giving up on seeing me again. I love you, and you are forever etched into the chambers of my heart.

Dubb,
My spirit had been crushed, and I saw myself in a broken image. You called me out and showed me how Heavenly Father sees me. Thank you. You are truly a gem in Papa's treasury.

Gary & Martha,
I can't keep myself from choking up. Any child would be honored & blessed to have you as their earthly parents. I remember the day I went knocking on your door. That door opened up a relationship for all eternity. Yahweh used you all as an instrument in saving my marriage to my beloved, and you showed me what unconditional love from parents looks like. Thank you for sharing things that were difficult for me to hear, and teaching me through your actions how to walk in a deeper relationship with the Lord. Thank you for taking our girls as your own and cherishing and loving them so. I love you, and I am thankful for you. May God bless you infinitely and abundantly more than you could ever think or imagine.

Apostles Mark & Patricia,
Here I go again…getting all choked up. There are no words to express the thoughts of my heart for you. I am thankful for your lives and the honor, love, truth, wisdom, counsel, revelation, and understanding you share not only into my

life, but, also into the lives of so many. Thank you for stretching me and calling me higher. There have been days when it was tough to hear course correction, but I am thankful for your integrity. I appreciate the late night and wee early morning calls. You are a dynamite duo and mega warriors of the Kingdom of God. I love and cherish you both as spiritual parents. Thank you for walking as beautiful image bearers of the Father. Thank you for pouring into me and others. May the Lord bless you infinitely of every seed sown!

Keith & Angela,
Thank you for caring. I see your hearts that give, give, and give even more. I am blown away by the crazy faith you live in. Thank you for showing me a different "sight" into the Kingdom of Heaven and the economy of Heaven. I had just about given up on something, and then the Lord used your encouragement to stretch me and pull me further. Thank you. I still see that "white house," and one day I know you will be blown away by the millions of lives changed because of what you have given and sacrificed. I appreciate and love you! God bless you both!

Apostle David,
I do not know if I have ever shared the story of what I said to the Lord in my heart before you spoke that first word from God's heart to me. If you only knew. I have so much gratitude for your words that pierce right through to the bullseye! You carry the Father's heart well, and love deeply. Thank you

for encouraging me to walk with boldness, fearless, and with fire. I pray that you and Dee experience the lavish love and blessings of the Father beyond your wildest dreams in this New ERA! You are a rockstar!

Apostle Alex & Jenny,
You are both incredible Warriors for Christ. You go after the deep things of the Lord, and you teach all of us how to maneuver in our prayer lives in the deep chambers of the Father's heart. Thank you for your love and keen insight. The Lord bless you both richly and abundantly.

Sir Clyde,
I do not know if you will ever know the impact you have had in so many lives across the globe. Thank you for walking me through the limitless possibilities with Yahweh. You helped me see that I was still carrying shackles that the Lord never intended for me to carry. They never belonged to me. Because of you, I grew in wisdom and understanding of civility and how to navigate treacherous systems and bring in the weighty glory of the Lord. God bless you, Sir Clyde.

I want to make a final mention of a wondrous woman I'll call "Kat". This project could not have come to completion without her. She is a woman full of love for God and country. She works tirelessly to make sure people are "awake" and "activated" in Christ and their "civic" duties. She is a bold woman of great faith that defies the world's narrative and refuses to take "no" for an answer. Kat, may God bless you richly in the years ahead, and may you reap seven-fold fruit of what you have sown into all of us.

Thank you!

FOREWORD

People have scars on the outside of their bodies from accidents and injuries. Others have scars on the inside that no one ever sees.

Silence can be a killer. It starts eating from within until there is nothing left to chew. Like termites gnawing their way through construction, the family doesn't know the toxic insects are eating away at the home's foundation until the outward damage is noticed. And then, from the mouth comes words you might wish you'd never said or heard spoken.

The good, the bad, and the downright ugly causes division, creates heartbreak and sometimes permanent separation from family and friends. Sadly, even a turn from faith tops the division list. Many hurting people will never break their silence for fear of condemnation, ridicule, mockery, and the concern that their story would fall on deaf ears or be dismissed as bunk. Some people go to their graves having held their silence for fear it would have cost them their life long before natural causes did.

I share *I Am Silent No More* because I have lived and learned how vitally important speaking the truth happens to be for the body, soul, mind and spirit and from a standpoint of faith.

Please join me on my journey from past to present. I have a lot of truths to tell.

~ *Lynz Piper-Loomis*

PREFACE

BEFORE BEGINNING THIS book I want to share with you an encounter with death—which haunted me—and how I learned to overcome because of Christ. If you suffer this same fear, it will stretch you. Before beginning my book, I want you to have a bit of grid regarding where I have come from and why I walk free today.

For years, death kept trying to take me out. Death chased after me, and wanted to glorify himself in any attempt he could to torture me, to steal from me, to destroy me, and yes…even kill me.

Tell me though…Death where is your sting? Death where is your victory? Oftentimes, I think Death is glorified way too much. Think about it. How expensive are funerals? How much do funeral directors get paid? Death is placed on the altar of victory (or the counterfeit false image of victory). Death is memorialized, and death is glorified.

My advice? Stop it.

You will find throughout my story how many times death came for me. I stand here today to tell you that it does not have to be that way. Death does not have the victory. The stone has been rolled away from the grave of Jesus. He has the victory! We are victorious through Him.

Before I get into a dream I had, let me preface: for years, I was petrified of "death". I was "deathly afraid" of death, darkness, funeral homes, dead bodies…anything death related. I hated it.

Four years ago I was asleep in my bed, which was positioned not far from my husband's empty hospital bed. His legs had been healed not long before this particular night. Though I was asleep, I was keenly aware that my body was sweating profusely and drenching my bed sheets. My body was shaking from the dream I will never forget. It was surreal.

In the encounter of my dream, I was walking into a funeral home for a service with my husband and two girls. People were standing around and talking. I looked over at the open casket on display, and I saw this shiny angelic being in a casket. I knew immediately something was off in my dream. The angelic being hopped out of the box, and I quickly discerned that it was the angel of "death."

I spoke my family out of the dream encounter, and the angel of death began to taunt me, mock me, and poke me physically. I was not shaken nor moved by his threats. I was keenly aware that my physical body in the bed turned completely cold, and I woke up with the angel of death at the foot of my bed. He was insidious and hideous looking. His presence could no longer steal my peace or faze me.

This time, I was ready for him when he came for me. I shot out of the bed and immediately told him, "The Lord rebuke you. Get behind me, Satan. I never knew you. If you do not fall down on your knees and recognize Jesus Christ of Nazareth that came here in the form of man, died, and resurrected from the grave, and is now seated at the right hand of the Father…I command you to leave."

You see, I learned as an overcomer that death has no victory in my life. **Death** has no sting. Death does not define me, and **death** definitely does not dictate my life.

I AM FREE!

CHAPTER ONE

I'D LOVE TO be able to share the details that led to my parents' divorce, but there is nothing my infant mind can recall about it. Of course, as I grew older, murmurings of what might have happened sort of served as missing pieces to an unfinished puzzle that had been boxed up and tucked away until a specified time determined by God.

What I do know about my father? He was a cowboy. I don't know where he was originally born because his father was in the military. Dad rode horses and moved cows in the cattle pins at the feed yards. Rumors were he liked to drink, but what cowboy didn't?

In most every divorce case, there is mudslinging, character assassinations, along with the conviction to prove one side is right while the other side is lying profusely and dead wrong with their words and actions. But there didn't seem to be a finger-pointing fight, not to my knowledge anyway.

When I was older, the one thing I do remember Mom telling me—that stuck—is she had spotted another woman's shoes in their house. At the time, I was too naïve to understand that finding another woman's shoes might indicate infidelity. Other than that statement, Mom never badmouthed my father out of concern for my safety. She protected me. I repeat—Mom always protected me.

Before I was even out of diapers, my parents had divorced, and my father had terminated his parental rights. That act on his part left a stain on my life along with a permanent question mark. So what if he drank? So what if he wasn't perfect? Who is? I was his biological daughter. Why would my Dad not want me? What did I do wrong? Would I ever understand or accept not having an answer as to why Dad terminated his parental rights of me?

Moving on is exactly what we did. To make life as a single mom a little easier, we relocated from Utah to Arizona. That way, we were not all by ourselves. Mom's family was in Arizona, so we were returning to her roots and to be geographically closer to family. Mom was very close with her grandmother, which was my great grandmother, Mary. I'll hereinafter refer to her as Great GranMary.

Though our maternal side of the family was very affluent—they owned farming, ranching, and trucking companies—Mom didn't rely on anyone for financial support. She was determined to make it on her own. I was probably approaching four years old, and Mom would get me from the bed at two or three o'clock in the morning so she could deliver newspapers at her paper route in Arizona.

In the wee hours of the morning, the stars all twinkling in position and the moon providing light in the nighttime sky, I recall lying in the back seat on stacks of newspapers. Mom would pull them out from under me before tossing them into yards or inserting them inside mailboxes.

During the day, she was a lab technician in the hospital. Mom was a hard worker and a strong Christian woman. Although I was her only child, she certainly didn't spoil me. Mom could rule with an iron fist, but she would never hurt me. She never physically or verbally abused me. I only got a handful of spankings, and it was with a wooden spoon. I felt a slight sting from the *pops*, but she never drew blood or caused any bruises. I never thought I'd laugh about it because when she got mad, it wasn't funny. But I was a quite a little chatter box, and one time Mom said, "Stifle it."

Sarcastically, I dared her, "Make me." And there went the pops against my skin from a wooden spoon. From that point on, I stifled it.

I remember her washing my mouth out with soap for talking back. You'd think I would have learned, but then that little temper I had would flare up again. Mom would tell me to clean up my room. Instead of obeying her, I would remove every single article of clothing from every single drawer and dump it in the middle of the floor. And I would hear Mom scream, "Lynz Nicole."

She had a slight temper, too. So if the mood struck the wrong way when she would ask me to do this, do that, stop doing this, stop doing that, I challenged her by intentionally defying her request, which led to us sometimes butting heads. Throughout it all, Mom could amazingly keep her cool and wits about her—even when I deserved to have my behind blistered.

Not to mention I was the kid that would stand on the handles of the doors in our rooms, and I would climb up on either side and do gymnastics. I hung off the clothes rack pole once, and it all fell down.

As good-natured, good-hearted and as sugary sweet as Mom was with my mischief, she was stern and could scare me as much as Miss Agatha Hennigan scared the orphans in the movie *Annie*. I quickly learned that when my momma would dart those dark eyes of hers my direction when I was misbehaving, I'd straighten up like a soldier frozen at attention. It spared Mom—and myself—from further reprimands.

Honestly, I was blessed if I got to watch the *Smurfs*. She was so strict about what I watched, how I dressed, and what I participated in. Later on, I came to understand why Mom was so protective.

While she worked two jobs, I led quite a privileged life. When it came to my maternal grandmother, money was never an issue. Grandma had a book of bank cards, and I remember us taking off for the mall to shop and dining in five star restaurants. My maternal grandparents had a very nice house. My grandfather was a police officer and a lover of the military. They sponsored the Air Force Cadets. Grandma and Grandpa entertained a lot. Their home seemed to be a revolving door of people coming in and out all the time. We had what they called soirees, which were evening parties where we would gather, eat and enjoy conversation and music at my grandparents' home. And we would congregate at the family farm every year.

When it came to money and togetherness, there was never any lack in that capacity. At such a young age, I didn't realize I was living the high-life. I simply thought fine living was normal, not a privilege. Grandma was very refined. I like to say she was "English-y." She made it her job to see that I had polite manners. She was as proper as the royal family. She taught me all the table settings, appropriate dining and etiquette before I started first grade. Even though I went along with it because I loved her, I despised all the prim and proper etiquette.

And those fluffy dresses she had me wear, I roll my eyes recalling the visuals. I was like...forget the royalty style of living. I would rather mount a horse and take off on a nature ride!

CHAPTER TWO

A S LOVELY AND lively as everything seemed, my spirit always picked up a dark side—a feeling of uneasiness and creepiness.

As nice and beautiful as the home of my grandparents, I remember being scared to close my eyes at night in the bedroom they had me sleep in at their house. They would always try to send me in the basement. Why? I don't know. But I can't express enough how much I hated stepping inside that area of the home.

As far back as I can recall, I could see in the Spirit. In my experience, I saw the demonic side of things first. As I grew in my relationship with the Lord, I began to see things in the light and how the light always overcomes the darkness, and then you see that manifest in the flesh.

My sentiments are fully supported by 1 Corinthians 2:10-15 where it is written: But God has revealed *them* to us through His Spirit. For the Spirit searches all things, yes, the deep things of God. For what man knows the things of a man except the spirit of the man which is in him? Even so no one knows the things of God except the Spirit of God. Now we have received, not the spirit of the world, the Spirit who is from God, that we might know the things that have been freely given to us by God. These things we also speak, not in words which man›s wisdom teaches but which the Holy Spirit teaches, comparing spiritual things with spiritual. But the natural man does not receive the things of the Spirit of God, for they are foolishness to him; nor can he know *them,* because they are spiritually discerned. But he who is spiritual judges all things, yet he himself is *rightly* judged by no one.

In those areas of my grandparents' house, there were so many demonic doors open—spiritually speaking. That is a memory I have with vivid recall.

The other memory, I sort of pushed it out of my mind. My grandma would make Grandpa meals and then bring his food to him on a tray, placing it on his lap in the chair where he'd sit and watch television. Sometimes, I would be sitting in his lap while he was waiting for Grandma to serve him, and he would start touching me. The exact places, I don't recall. I do know it was underneath my skirt or my dress, and I can tell you it was inappropriate. It made me feel so uncomfortable and beyond icky.

When I see little girls make a squeamish face when a certain political figure hugs or touches them publicly—or as much as sniffs their hair—I can relate. I wanted to remove Grandpa's hand from my body—send him the message that I wasn't okay with his touching me. Or either instruct, "Grandpa…Stop. This is gross." Instead, I said nothing.

It was always the love Momma gave me—along with her unyielding protection—that made everything in life right, no matter what had gone wrong. Yet it seemed from the time I was little, Satan had been after the life of my momma and myself.

Both animal lovers, we had dogs, cats, birds, parrots, chickens, and horses.

As far as dogs, Mom's Golden Retriever named Sandy was stolen from her. So then she got Sammy. And Sammy, for some reason, didn't like me. He growled at me a lot because I probably provoked him. I was little. He bit me in the face, and I still wear the slight scar, yet it was my own fault. Momma had warned, "Don't get near Sammy's face." What did I do? I got near his face and got bit.

We had a couple of cats that we rescued: Tugboat and Steamboat. Steamboat was Mom's cat. I claimed Tugboat for myself. Mom had an affinity for animals, and she made me a lover of them as well. We could never say no to rescues. If Facebook had been around in the 90s, we would have taken every dog and cat in need and provided shelter. Around Christmas of one year, she got a German

Shepherd and named her Noel. I loved how my mother tied the holiday season in with naming the puppy.

I still love and own dogs, but I have such a heart for horses. Omigosh! I love positioning my feet in the stirrups, mounting the horse, and taking off for a galloping ride. These creatures of beauty teach us about ourselves. Not only that, I love the sense of adventure, the freedom and the empowerment riding a horse brings to my soul and spirit. I even love the feel of the breeze, and my hair blowing in the wind when riding.

But we did have this one particular horse that went to the stable. He was an Appaloosa named Agitator. Ironically titled as that's exactly what Agitator could sometimes be. People used to always ask, "What is it with Agitator?" We never quite figured out his problem.

I was around three years old, and Mom and I had gone horseback riding. We were on a trail and something spooked him. Agitator threw us off. Momma's head hit a rock. I landed in between her legs. As for me, I was only scuffed up. But she was knocked unconscious and had to be transported to the hospital via ambulance. Sutured behind her ear were forty stitches—quite a cut. As little as I was, I was frightened out of my wits that something bad had happened to my mother, and if it had, how would I live without her.

When she was discharged from the hospital, I was so relieved. I remember her sleeping on my grandma and grandpa's sofa, and I slept on a pallet on the floor beside her. I can recall my face sticking to the pillow with all the Neosporin where I had been scratched up and my face coming off the pillow and ripping the skin. Thank goodness, we both fully recovered.

CHAPTER THREE

YET IT SEEMED for every good thing that happened, something bad followed. Or perhaps it was just life. Whatever the case, I was experiencing my fair share far in advance of most kids my age. I'd bet many had never even heard of a funeral. I was probably three when I experienced my first one. I remember sitting on Momma's lap and seeing my great grandfather—my Great GranMary's husband—lying in an open casket. Death is the one thing in life that is certain. No one is going to escape it. I learned that at a young age.

Aside from having my maternal grandparents, I was fortunate enough to have and to know my maternal great grandparents, too, even though my great grandfather's death robbed me of spending more time with him.

My Great GranMary was awesome. She was incredibly sweet and kind to me always—and to everyone. When I would go to her house, I would bang on her piano. I had no knowledge of the seven natural notes—C, D, E, F, G, A, B—but I could hammer those keys. All that noise I made, and Great GranMary couldn't have cared less. That fact alone let me know how much she adored me!

She loved to collect teapots and tea cups, and I know she passed that passion along to my mother because Mom was a fanatic and an accumulator of them as well. The memories of their fondness for teapots and tea cups—for reasons good and bad—are forever stapled to my mind.

When I was four, we were at Great GranMary's house. She was sitting on the sofa holding a cup of tea. I was playing on the floor because I remember the coffee table being in front of me and the couch. She had a plastic cover on the couch to keep it from getting dirty because, God forbid, even a speck of dust would send "Mrs. Clean and Proper" into orbit. Every single item in her home had its appropriate place, and you didn't try to move or rearrange anything. That was a definite no-no.

While I was playing in the floor, Great GranMary set her cup of tea down on the coffee table. Then she sat back. No more talking. No more nothing. Her eyes no longer had life in them—only a fixed stare.

Momma noticed and asked, "Hey, GranMary! Are you okay?"

She brought her down to the floor and called 9-1-1. While waiting on the ambulance to arrive, Momma performed CPR on her...crying uncontrollably while trying to breathe life back into my Great GranMary.

It's odd some of the things you recall in a moment of crisis and other things you completely forget that happened. I remember Great GranMary lived in a really nice condo-style townhouse, much like California homes with the red clay roofs. She had two doors, and I remember going and opening the main door for the paramedics. They hurried inside and rushed her off to the hospital. I was heartbroken, but Momma was devastated when they pronounced her dead.

What's funny and touching: I drove Great GranMary crazy banging on her piano, and that is an item of value that she left me. Mom enrolled me in piano lessons, and I finally learned to play notes instead of all that heavy banging that echoed throughout the home like a boisterous piano playing permanently off-key.

She died in 1986. I won't forget because following the loss of Great GranMary, I gained a friend for life.

We were very involved with church, and Mom took me to Sunday School. One particular Sunday morning, the door was half-opened, half-closed. A man was just sitting in front of me, and I was in awe. He didn't speak, but I felt an overwhelming amount of warmth. I remember communicating, but not in the way I speak with everyday people. He had brown, wavy hair. And those eyes of his were mesmerizing. It's almost like the ocean roar in his eyes. And the frequency of his presence was so powerful. The way he smiled at me, I knew that He loved me. They were precious moments I've treasured.

When Mom came to the Sunday School room door to get me, I was so excited to talk to her and tell her about what happened. Outside the door, I exclaimed, "Mommy! Mommy! I gave my life to Jesus."

She knelt down on one knee—and I don't recall exactly what she said—but I think she was trying to see if I understood what I was talking about, basically. And I told her, "I asked Jesus into my heart."

And from that moment on—since I was around four years old—I've always known Jesus is with me. Even growing up, people would ask, "When did you invite Jesus into your life?" And I would say, "When I was four." I told everybody I came into contact with about my encounter with Christ. I was so proud of that moment and time with my Lord and Savior.

Have I had moments when I would look back and ask myself, *Did that Sunday School encounter really happen, or was it a figment of my imagination?*

Yes. I have asked myself those questions. And years later, it would be confirmed. It definitely happened!

CHAPTER FOUR

SOMEWHERE, BETWEEN OUR debacle on the horse and the death of Great GranMary, Mom met, dated and later married Bart, and he adopted me.

Being more of a farm girl, Mom wanted to relocate so we moved outside of the city, where we had been living, and moved into the country on five acres of land.

Bart had a mobile home that I will never forget because in my mind, I saw it as a sinking banana. Of course, it wasn't literally sinking; that's just how I saw it as a kid. But it was this gosh-awful bright yellow.

Behind the "Sinking Banana," they built a really nice house. Bart had his own business and was successful. Mom didn't have to work so hard—no more delivering newspapers—which gave her more time to spend with me. Time and togetherness are such blessings!

When we moved to the country, she put me in a public school. I had previously been in a private Christian school. But Momma ripped me out of the public system and put me back in Christian learning faster than you could blink when she found out the teacher was educating students on evolution and that we came from monkeys. She wasn't having any part of that, nor was she going to allow me to be led to believe such a thing.

I just can't express it enough, but my mom really raised me up in the Lord. We were very involved with church and various other things. At church functions, she sang. She had a beautiful voice. I can sing, too, but my voice was not the same as hers.

Another bonus is she was excellent in the kitchen. Any dish she whipped up was delicious. I attempted cooking, but I shudder at the recollections. When it came to culinary skills, it was disastrous. I honestly think—if I went back and counted—I had a total of seventeen kitchen fires trying to prepare meals. Let me tell you…it was bad.

Back to the home front with Bart, I never felt loved by him. In fact, I felt more of a burden or a nuisance. I can't recall one time Bart ever hugged me or told me that he loved me. Perhaps he did love me and I just never knew, but he certainly didn't say or do anything to show he cared about me in any fashion.

He played softball, and we would go to his games. While Momma watched him, I would entertain myself on the playground. One time I climbed up on those big canister trashcans to get to the monkey bars, and I fell into the trashcan. Don't ask me how that happened. It was just a freak accident. But that's the mischief that I sometimes got myself into. Kids will be kids. But Bart was irate with me because I had been injured. I always felt like I was nothing but a pain to him.

The glass cut open my chin. Of course, it was Momma who took care of me as I got no sympathy from Bart. And I still sport a scar on the right side of my face between my lip and chin. I carried emotional scars from how angry Bart became over the accident, but those inside scars eventually healed.

I likened myself to Amelia Bedelia, the clumsy, silly and sometimes mischievous storybook character. Oftentimes, I would go over to Rene's house—that was Mom's best friend—and I'd play with her kids. We would run around barefoot.

One time I rode a bicycle, and I went up the wooden ramp without shoes on. Of course, they told me to wear shoes, but "Amelia Bedelia" here didn't follow instructions. The failure to pay attention resulted in me getting these long splinters on the bottom of my feet from the big, thick planks. Talk about pain. I cringe when I recall that incident.

I was on an adrenaline rush—not because of the pain—but because Momma was coming to pick me up, and I knew I was going to be in so much trouble. Sitting atop the bathroom counter in a panic over how she would punish me, Rene assured me, "Stop worrying. We'll get these out."

And after Rene removed all the splinters and applied hydrogen peroxide, I slid on a pair of socks and shoes and walked to the car as if nothing had ever happened when, in actuality, I wanted to face-plant due to the unbearable pain in my feet. I don't think Momma ever found out about that incident. I faked it pretty well. Rene was so cool. She knew how strict my mother was so she covered for me. I was not a bad child, but I was extremely curious and adventuresome.

CHAPTER FIVE

THEN ONE DAY— out of the clear blue—for reasons still unknown to me, my biological father came to Bart and Mom's house with his new wife—my stepmom—his son, which would be my half-brother.

They brought gifts from his family. I remember a journal with a lock and stuff on it. More than the gift, I couldn't shake the feeling of awkwardness. The sight of seeing my biological father caused a well of emotions to spring up.

I always had feelings of abandonment and rejection, not just from Bart, but because my biological father terminated his parental rights of me. And somewhere between the ages of eight and ten, he showed up at the "Sinking Banana" with a journal.

I did have a lot of questions about him as I got older, and I queried my mom as to why my biological father showed up at our house after being absent from my life. She told me she would one day explain more.

Reflecting back, it's kind of funny. What is the irony of giving me a journal and me one day writing the twists and turns of my life? Maybe Dad knew in advance I'd need a lot of paper to pen my inside wounds. Interesting too, that the journal had a lock on it, but I've thrown away the key. There is nothing to hide anymore.

As for Mom and Bart's marriage, I can't describe it as good or bad. Like I mentioned previously, she never badmouthed my biological father or my stepdad. We did things as a family unit, but I never felt a part of Bart's life.

Was she happily married to Bart? I don't know. If she wasn't, she put up a good front. Then again— I'd later learn—Mom was skilled at mastering a front. Written words aren't always necessary. Time reveals the truth.

I do have one good memory that stands out of the two of them having fun together. They were in the bedroom and Bart was tickling her, and she was laughing herself silly. That's the only giddy mood and type of snickering I remember them sharing. So perhaps during their better times, I was not around. I could have been outside playing, at a friend's house, at school, or elsewhere. I just don't recall their relationship as a good, solid marriage filled with love and laughter.

However, I give Bart credit for providing. On top of the five acres we lived on, he had a timeshare in Hawaii. I enjoyed getting to go there when it was available and admiring the beauty of their beaches. But there is a quote, "Wherever you go, there you are." It's so true. Wherever I went, that heavy weight of abandonment and rejection hung from my neck like a bowling ball, but my momma served as the scale of balance.

CHAPTER SIX

IN OUR COMMUNITY, we were plugged in to so many things. I did some sewing and other projects—just not too much cooking. When it came to my school, Mom was actively involved and went on all the field trips. She was the leader of my 4H-Club and never missed a scholastic book fair. And she was so easy to talk to; everybody loved her.

She had become a Stephen Minister, which is a lay care ministry that offers pastoral care by teaching laypersons to provide one-on-one support to individuals who request it. By becoming a Stephen Minister, she touched so many lives.

In her Bible, she coined and carried a quote and recited it to me often, "Through our pain, it's an opportunity for someone else to gain."

And then the day came when I truly understood why Momma sealed that quote in her Bible and held it so close to her heart. It was as clear as spring water why she had become a Stephen Minister and was so heavily involved with helping other people. First and foremost, though, that's just who and how she was. But I can't express enough how high her passions ran.

In the year 1990, her brother, who was four years older than her, died from alcohol poisoning. But the real tragedy occurred after his death. While I carried around the weight of abandonment and rejection, Momma had her own inside scars.

When she was a child, she was sexually assaulted by her brothers and by her father. If that wasn't enough, she was forced to have sexual relations *with* her brothers *while* her own father watched. And there was severe physical abuse in the home as well. She had no one to protect or defend her, so she was basically raised up with an enormous amount of undealt-with trauma.

That being said, after her brother died, she told me what happened and literally said to me, "I'm not going to stay silent anymore." Mom spoke publicly about what had happened to her, unleashing the flood gates from all of her sexual and childhood abuse.

From those beginnings came a lot of endings, but not all were bad because Momma had ended her mental anguish and emotional pain by speaking the truth.

Everything started coming into focus for me. That explained why Momma had been so protective of me, sometimes a little too much. It made me wonder even more about my biological father? Was he a bad man? Or was it that Mother was so concerned, after they'd divorced, that what happened to her could possibly happen to me—during his visitation periods—if she wasn't present to protect me? I have no doubt her trust issues registered off the chart.

After knowing the truth, I'm sure it took everything within her power to stomach being in the presence of her own blood relatives. I truly believe—looking back—she did the majority of it for me and to keep the family intact. Like most everyone else, I'm certain she was hoping the wound would heal itself without the need for a public bleed. But healing doesn't work that way. Jesus bled publicly for the sins of all mankind.

A public bleed—whether it is the shedding of real blood or the soul finally screaming out from physical, mental, and emotional torture—is necessary in order for healing to occur.

All the while—at every family gathering— Momma was probably boiling on the inside but appeared so chill outwardly. Once I found out what she had lived through, I was completely baffled at how she interacted with such kindness and respect toward the family. Then again, it wasn't surprising. That was the genuineness of my mom.

People can disguise deep, dark secrets by making home and family life look like it's surrounded by canisters of love constantly setting off sweet fragrances when the truth actually carries a rigor mortis-type stench. I had learned so much in such a short amount of time. And, oh boy, was I heartbroken—for my momma and every ounce of pain she had endured.

Thoughts of my grandparents' basement flashed back. My heart raced at the visuals running through my mind. Was Momma molested in my grandparents' basement? Is that the reason I hated that area of their home so much? I wanted no part of it whatsoever. I could see the darkness when I hadn't even opened the door. My insides trembled at the very thought of even setting my foot on the first step that led to their downstairs. It was demonic, but I knew that long before the family secret was outed.

And the way Grandpa made me feel, too, was nauseating. The thoughts were coming at me like a tsunami that wouldn't stop. When Grandpa placed his hand under my skirt and dress and touched me, it *was* inappropriate. I had picked up on his sick and ick long before I knew about Mom's horrific experiences.

I'll probably repeat this phrase numerous times: The spirit always knows before the flesh. I knew Grandpa's behavior—when I was sitting in his lap—was beyond gross; I had to stop myself from thinking or it was going to drive me insane.

Needless to say, when Momma came forward and spoke the truth, it was literally like an explosion of dynamite had been set off. The whole family split. Mom cut off all communication with her biological father. Her other brother quit talking to her.

I was told my grandmother knew it was going on, but she did nothing about it. We can sweep dust under the carpet, but it only builds into a larger pile of dirt. Not long after the blast of the family secret, my grandmother and grandfather divorced. We became estranged from the entire family. It was a wicked fiasco from start to finish, but Mom had to empty out her garbage in order for her soul and spirit to be cleansed.

Through her brother's death from alcohol poisoning, Mom finally gathered the courage to release the toxins she'd buried and carried inside of her for years. As difficult as it was, I was so proud of her for regurgitating the truth.

CHAPTER SEVEN

FOR EVERY SUBTRACTION from my life, an addition followed. A man named Robert Starling lived in Lilly Valley, Arizona, the town where Mom was born. He owned a large ranch, and he was very well known throughout the entire nation for angus cattle and quarter horses. After the family split, Robert Starling basically became like a father to my mom and a grandfather to me. I even referred to him as "Grandpa Starling." He filled a void from the absence of what was once a large family unit shattered by abuse and deception.

He was quite the catch. Being a widow and having lots of money, most every woman in town and beyond wanted to date him. Funny thing is I don't recall him dating anyone. He seemed satisfied and content being alone. Or if he did date, he kept his personal business private.

If he were still alive today, I'd love to throw my arms around him and offer a huge, heartfelt hug. I'd tell him what a great male role model he was and how he impacted my life in ways he never knew and left me with the fondest of memories. I can't put enough emphasis on the fact that

Grandpa Starling was the first man in my life who was absolutely amazing.

Being a lover of animals and nature himself, he got me my sheep. And I remember him telling me, "Don't get emotionally attached to them." That was like telling a dog lover not to rescue the lost puppy. I love sheep. If only I'd listened to Grandpa Starling. Instead, I did the exact opposite from what he'd instructed. I became so attached, I wanted to pick them up and hold them in my arms like a baby.

Grandpa Starling took Mom and me to the Magnolia County Fair. And when it came time to load the sheep on the truck, I was crying uncontrollably. In fact, I was in the pin on my knees with my arms wrapped around them screaming, "Noooo."

They had to pull me off of them. The sheep had been auctioned off, and I was devastated that someone else was taking them. I could see the shock on Mom's face. She was so upset about me being traumatized. I'll never forget that day and how it ripped my heart out to see the sheep I had grown to care for and love being hauled off by someone I didn't know and didn't trust could ever love them as much as I did.

It was a hard lesson, but I learned why Grandpa Starling had warned me not to become emotionally attached to those sheep.

But then there was a ewe—a female lamb—
who had been under market so she couldn't go.
Her name was Ya Katarina. Mom and Grandpa
Starling went and bought her and gave her to
me. God bless the two of them for helping to
mend my broken heart. They said that I could
use her and make her a pet. She was going to
become a breeding ewe. I called her Katie for
short. She was a Suffolk sheep. Grandpa Starling
said the best sheep were Suffolk sheep, and he
would know.

But one wasn't enough. We got Katie a pal—
another ewe. But she was a Colombia sheep, and
she wasn't very nice. She didn't like me. Perhaps
she was jealous because she knew I favored
Katie, who became my baby and followed me
everywhere. Animals are like people; they have
feelings, too.

Mom had gotten a new horse—a Paint horse—
that she named Jado. Paint horses are great for
beginners and loyal to their owners. Smart and
able to catch on quickly, they were used by Native
Americans. They are very docile.

At that same time, I was excited to have my first
year of showing my sheep in the school's 4-H
Club. Grandpa Starling had helped train me. "If
you're moving from side to side, don't ever go
around the back of the lamb and never turn your
back to the lamb. Set your animal up in a way
that you want the judge to see it. Show the judge

the best view of your animal." Grandpa Starling had the instructions down.

Knowing they were going to market, I named them "Short Circuit" and "Johnny 5" from the movie *Short Circuit,* which is about an experimental robot getting electrocuted in a lab. Even though it was released in 1986, I won't give the rest of the story away for those who might want to watch it. It was one of my favorite films as a child.

It's sad to admit, but spending time with Grandpa Starling was heavenly, and then having to go back home to Bart was hell.

Outside the steps of the Sinking Banana—what I'd nicknamed the yellow mobile home—there were these concrete steps. And for reasons I don't even recall, Bart got mad at me. There was like a concrete slab and three or four steps. Oh, man! He grabbed me by the nape of my neck and threw me down those steps. Aside from a sore elbow, I wasn't physically harmed, but I was hurting emotionally from the incident.

Plain and simple: Bart was not nice. In fact, he was downright mean to me. Even though he did adopt me, I truly believe my mom pushed his action so that at least on paper, I would have a father.

Once he threw me down the steps, I didn't feel safe around him anymore. Besides, I knew he wasn't my real dad, and so I never felt accepted, only rejected three thousand times over. The feelings of betrayal were something I could never shake. He didn't talk kindly to me. He never showed affection—like a father gives to a child—so I knew he didn't love me.

Basically, I felt like an unwanted kid in his house. In fact, he always isolated himself from me. If I came into the room, he either left or ignored me. So, yeah, Bart was there as a figure-head for a father, but he was never present for me. I thank God for Grandpa Starling. He was the father/grandfather figure who brought nothing but joy into my world.

As I mentioned, I was involved in all kinds of activities with church and school. I was also in the Awanas—child discipleship—when I was a kid. I did everything. I was always very active. I played the piano, and I was very good for someone my age. For the most part, I enjoyed it, but it was the practicing that I dreaded.

CHAPTER EIGHT

S PEAKING OF THE activities, there was a musical at church called *Let's Go to the Rock*—a 50s musical that Mom and I were in. What stood out most were the 50s skirts we wore, and I still have some of the lyrics to the songs memorized, which is quite good for the musical having been such a long time ago now—September 18th, 1994 to be exact.

There is a very valid reason to remember. Five days prior, I had turned twelve years old. Because I'd mouthed off, Mom canceled the birthday party she'd planned for me. A few days later, I guess guilt got the best of her because after the musical, she took me to Red Robin—one of my favorite restaurants.

I still didn't get the honor of having my friends join us because I was grounded for having been rude. So it was just Mom and me having ice cream and cake together to celebrate what was then a belated birthday. Even though I didn't get to spend my birthday with my friends, I had fun alone with Mom.

All of that leads me to the following day—one I'll never forget—September 19th, 1994.

After at a 4-H meeting in Magnolia Forest, I remember walking out of the gathering and a friend said, "Let's go play ball."

Mom overheard and said, "Don't run off because we need to get home."

We had our meetings at a local church, which I found funny because Mom could never separate herself from church services and activities. She was talking to someone, and I ran after the ball—something she caught me doing out of the corner of her eye. And she hollered, "Lynz, let's go."

We got into her new car—a gray Ford Taurus—that she was so proud to own after trading out her Chevy Celebrity that had the red velvet seats. It had been her dad's car, so she was so glad to be rid of it and excited about her fairly new Ford Taurus.

The drive home was only about twenty to thirty minutes. Sitting in the front passenger seat, I remember having a discussion that was out of the ordinary. I asked Mom, "If I got pregnant before I got married, would you still love me?"

And she replied, "Lynz, haven't I always loved you. I love you now and I always will."

I wasn't having sex or too interested in boys yet. I had just turned twelve. That's why asking Mom that question was so strange.

As we approached the intersection, she stopped. There wasn't a traffic light. And I didn't count how many times she looked left and then looked right, but it was quite a number of times. She wanted to make certain the coast was clear before turning left onto Magnolia Road because there happened to be a little bit of a hill, which made for a blind spot.

She was turning left when a car, heading over that blind hill, actually came into our lane. It didn't hit the back door or her front wheel. It slammed directly into the driver's door.

Mom saw the oncoming car because right before impact, she braced and put her hand across my chest to try and shield me.

The vehicle struck us with such force, it spun Mom's Ford Taurus across to the other side of the road and onto a field. Of course, I don't remember everything, but I do recall bits and pieces. I was wearing a seatbelt, but my head hit the dash. I can't exactly explain how this happened, but I was tiny and my body did some type of flipping mechanism inside of that seat.

The next thing I remember was feeling the overwhelming presence of God. I was walking toward Heaven with Momma when, suddenly, I stopped. My mother stopped in her tracks as well. I turned around, and God showed me what my destiny held. It wasn't spoken aloud by Him; it was a message I understood the Lord conveying to me in the spirit—that I had a governmental call on my life. I didn't understand the depth and gravity of it, but I understood I had a choice. I don't know how to best explain the unusual encounter other than to say I knew in that moment—in the spiritual sphere—that my life would be a part of history. And we all are, obviously.

Having been born into a military family, it would only make sense and be fitting because in my earlier years, I was surrounded by US Air Force servicemen. I loved America and studying its history. Born and bred an American, I've always showed patriotism and loyalty to my country— even at a very young age.

So there I was facing a tough decision. I could choose to stay with Momma and go into Heaven— and there was no shame or condemnation either way—or I could continue my life on Earth. Also in that moment—as weird as it sounds—I understood that Mom understood she wasn't coming back, but that the purpose of her life was to prepare me for what I was called to do.

It was like this unspoken messaging of the minds between God, Momma, and myself.

Personally and spiritually, I knew I had no choice. I turned around, went to my mother, and I hugged her goodbye. After I bid my momma a final farewell, I felt the weight and the presence of the glory of God.

And then I woke up in excruciating pain—my whole darn body. My screaming cries were that of a helpless, torturous, hurt and agony.

When God blew his breath back into my being—after my encounter with death—first responders were on the scene cutting a hole into the side of my chest cavity and inserting a tube because I had a collapsed lung and couldn't breathe. When they cut my side and put the tube in, I felt relief and a release.

I turned my head toward the driver's seat. The memory of Mom's arms still being right next to me as I was being extricated is forever etched in my mind. Her head was hit; her neck was snapped, but I didn't see one drop of blood on her. Her lifeless body lay still while her spiritual body was very much alive and in a better place. Contrary to what anyone might think or say, I know where she was because I'd walked her to the front door of Heaven—a real paradise where I can't wait to spend eternity.

Once they cut me out of the car, I was placed on a stretcher. I can't recall the exact order because I had been in and out of consciousness, but as they were transporting me toward the ambulance, I have a memory of a body bag that I was certain they'd use to place the remains of my sweet and loving mother.

No one ever wants to bid their mom or a loved one farewell. But I realized after the accident and autopsy that if she had survived, she probably would have been in a coma for the rest of her life. It was complete impact to her head.

I was rushed to Memorial Hospital and admitted to Children's ICU. I had a head injury; blood had clotted around my brain. I fractured my neck. My collar bone was broken on the left side. At least nine of my ribs were broken. My pelvic bone was broken in two places. Aside from that, I had many other broken bones. I suffered massive internal bleeding. My reproductive organs were severely damaged. My heart was damaged, my liver, my spleen, my lung.

After being put through intensive examinations, sutured and wrapped in casts, I was finally admitted to a room. One of Mom's best friends, Auntie Rose was present and holding my right hand. I saw Jesus standing at the head of me, and Mom was holding my left hand. All three were praying over me. People would argue that I was hallucinating, but I know what I saw.

As much as I hurt physically and as scarred as I was emotionally, I had peace in that moment. But during the time I was in the hospital, my attitude changed. No one would acknowledge anything about Mom or that she was gone—even though I knew she was. I became livid.

Laying there beaten, battered, and broken from one end of my body to the other, I was really mean to all of my nurses. I bit them; I kicked them. I was in major trauma. My Aunt Ursula—Mom's sister—told me to behave, that they were trying to take care of me. But I was outraged at everybody because not a single member of my family would talk about my mom being gone.

Then they had the nerve to try and convince me that she'd pulled out in front of the car that struck us and caused the accident. And I shouted, "No. That's not what happened."

Before the accident—because of the blind hill—I vividly recall how Momma kept looking left and looking right multiple times before she proceeded. But all the people who weren't even at or near the accident scene were trying to tell me the accident was Momma's fault. That is just not true. My fury grew stronger than hurricane winds.

Just when I thought it would never be mentioned, Bart came into the hospital room with the doctors and said, "Lynz, your mom died in the accident." I just glared at him and said, "Finally, someone told me. I know she's gone. I could have told you that."

And don't ask me where this came from, but I blurted out, "When I bust out of here, I'm going to start cooking some really good meals." I'm sure I said that because I knew Mom was an outstanding cook and I wasn't. But I'd darn sure try to match her skills in the kitchen so Bart could enjoy some decent food. Perhaps I thought it would make him like me and treat me with the respect I deserved.

And then there was my biological father that my family had me speak with via phone. When he started telling me how much he loved me, it only accelerated my anger. In a normal state and within the bounds of a functional family, I would have been reeling with joy and flattered to have heard my biological father say, "I love you" to me. If the dysfunction wasn't enough, the family planned Mom's funeral on a Friday, one day *before* I was discharged from the hospital. Bart's family came into town for her service. Afterward, they came to the hospital and showed me pictures of Mom in her casket. Not only did I feel that was mean and rude, it showed such a lack of compassion. She didn't look like herself at all. The clothes they had put on her didn't match any outfits I'd ever seen her wear. They videoed Mom's funeral, but they didn't want to show it to me for some reason.

Feeling alone and helpless fuels anger all the more.

Reflecting back, how could I not be furious at the world and everybody in it? My body was in a mess. Emotionally, I was a wreck. They were trying to pin the accident on Mom, and it wasn't her fault. I saw the car coming into our lane.

I was one mad child, missing my mother immensely, mad that she wasn't there to defend herself and already worrying and wondering who would love and take care of me now that the most important and loving person was gone. Devastated could never begin to describe how huge my loss was and how frustrated I was that—just because I survived—nobody could feel or understand the pain and grief that had a chokehold on me internally and externally.

With nothing to do but lie in a hospital bed and think while I recovered, I reflected back to the days leading up to the accident. Mom was acting strange. She was making comments like, "If anything ever happens to me, this is where Lynz should go."

Never before had she ever talked like that, and I remember how much it had disturbed me. Hearing her speak in that manner was strange, and it gave me an eerie feeling. It wasn't like Mom—a Stephen Minister— to be talking doom. She was always the light in the darkness. Even though she had been a victim of sexual molestation at the hands of her own kin, she was a survivor.

Too, it wasn't that Mom was so broken that she didn't want to be alive anymore. Bart and Mom had a timeshare in Hawaii, and we were scheduled to go as a family in November. She was excited about our upcoming vacation. In short, Mom was not suicidal and no one ever suggested that she was.

That being said, one of her favorite things to do was berry picking. Her second favorite thing to do was to eat at Rambo's, a pizza restaurant where your number would show up on the mirror when your pizza was ready. The other cool thing about Rambo's was listening to their pianola, a piano that would play without anyone touching it.

Earlier in the week, we had gone berry picking and to Rambo's, two of Mom's favorite things— almost as if she knew her time on Earth would be cut short. Most importantly, though, I was baptized the day before she died. It was a sprinkling—not a full dunk at that church.

And, why, just moments before impact, had I asked Mom if she would still love me if I got pregnant outside of wedlock? I wasn't having sexual relations with any man. I was only twelve years old, and I didn't even have a boyfriend.

As strict as Mom was, I knew if I slipped up and became pregnant before marrying, that would infuriate her. In my twelve year old mind, becoming pregnant might have been the worst possible action I could take to make her mad enough to fall out of love with me.

In retrospect, I came to the realization that Mom was about to permanently leave this Earth, and I needed to hear that she loved me before she departed. God allowed me that opportunity, and gave me a treasured memory that has carried me throughout life without her.

If anything positive resulted from the accident, a traffic light was installed at that intersection not long afterward. And that's about as much credit as I could give to finding any silver lining from that fateful day. My mom died so the lives of others might be saved.

It wasn't just the traffic light that saved lives. I do recall one other thing that stood out in my mind from Mom's funeral. A man attended, who had never before set foot in a church. And he was so touched over the death of my Mom and enamored with the inside of the sanctuary that he dedicated his life to Christ.

I realized after the accident that if Momma had survived, she probably would have been in a coma for the rest of her life. So I'd rather she be healed, whole and home. She would never have wanted to live in a vegetative state.

It's God's miracle, I survived. I should have died, too. Well, I actually did and God brought me back. It took a year to heal and for the blood to dissolve from around the brain.

Some things are left untouched and unspoken. Curious, I went back and read the autopsy report several years later. Though I cannot prove any kind of criminal intent, I'll never have complete peace about the accident. Maybe that's normal coping mechanism or being in survival mode after a tragedy. But in my gut, I've always felt something sinister surrounded that accident. The question is: will I ever really know?

Throughout life, memories of the trauma come and go. It was, and still is, something incredibly powerful. And it's actually the driving force behind everything I do, the determination to pick myself up by the boot straps and keep going no matter how tough the journey.

CHAPTER NINE

FOR SOMEONE AS injured as I had been, I recovered really well. Within two weeks from the accident, I was able to leave the hospital. It was a Saturday. I remember because I'd missed Mom's funeral on the Friday before. Thankfully, there was a memorial service for her the following Monday at the church.

I had left the hospital in a wheelchair, but I walked myself down to the front of the church for Mom's memorial service. I was shaking—still in shock. Mom loved Sandy Patty. And even in the shape I was in, I managed to sit down at the piano and play a Sandy Patty song in her honor. Gordon, a friend of Mom's, played the bagpipes. It warmed my heart to see the sanctuary and the hallways filled with so many people who'd poured in to show their love and respect for Momma.

Popular and well-loved in the community, but an unknown in the global world, it's uncanny that I've always compared Mom's death to Princess Diana's accident. In fact, when the media reported that the Princess of Wales had succumbed to her injuries, I cried as if I was reliving our entire accident all over again. I could feel every bit of separation, emotion and heartbreak William and

Harry were suffering. Like myself, William and Harry were too young to lose their mother—and so tragically. No goodbye. No hand-holding. No hugs. No kiss on the cheek. Just like that...gone in a blink.

I'm sure everyone was certain I'd wail like never before at the service. But you know what? I didn't. I think it might have blown the minds of the people who expected me to fall apart because—well, it even shocked me.

Having spent only two weeks in the hospital from all of those extensive bodily injuries and being pumped full of different medications is probably one reason I didn't have a complete meltdown. Secondly, I was my mom's sidekick, always with her. We were like conjoined twins, so I really don't think it had completely set in that she was gone.

After the memorial service, I kept trying to be the good girl and fight my anger. But every time I tried to suppress it, I literally thought I was going to break into werewolf mode. I wanted to tell everyone, "I'm not okay. I'm a train wreck. I miss my mother. I'm not comfortable living at Bart's. He doesn't give a crap about me. My biological father relinquished his parental rights. The maternal side of our family is separated by the sins of the father and brothers. Can someone PLEASE understand me?"

But, no, I couldn't say that out loud. And if I did, no one would have heard or understood. Sometimes it felt like their attitude was: "You survived. Get over it. And P.S. Forget your mother died in the crash."

Even though Mom had become the black sheep of the family once she'd divulged her brothers and father had molested her as a child shortly after the oldest brother passed away, I still have no doubt that my grandmother, my aunt, Bart, and all the rest of the family were emotionally ripped inside as well over the loss of Momma.

Not everyone grieves the same. Surely, they had to be hurting, too. But instead of receiving love from them and just simply having someone listen, support and encourage me, their behavioral response was more like a foreign language the family never learned to speak. Just epic communication failures that led to destruction, and their rejection and abandonment of me.

For instance, I remember being really upset and crying out for Mom, and she didn't come. That caused me to have horrific nightmares. The flashbacks of the incident played repeatedly in my head. Instead of consoling me, the family tried to keep me silent. The more I couldn't communicate, the angrier I became.

Thank God for the wonderful people at Mom's church. They were kind and attentive to my needs. They brought meals, spent good quality time with me and listened. I considered them my real family.

CHAPTER TEN

WHILE I WAS trying to pick up the pieces from my shattered world, nothing felt right anymore. Things weren't the same. I was already starting to be cut off from people.

Living with Bart was just as I expected. He paid no attention to me, never consoled me, and I felt so all alone. To try to escape the insanity in my head—reliving the car accident, the recovery, the memorial service—I became like a drifter because he forced me out.

I went and I stayed with my grandma, but I wasn't there very long—maybe two weeks. And I remember her telling me, "This isn't going to work. I just can't do this."

I was living on and off the street. Then I'd spend a couple of weeks with different friends, and their parents would say I had to go home. I was a living mess trying to survive a living mess.

Back to Bart's I went. Mom hadn't been in the ground two months, and he already had a girlfriend. I held so much resentment when he brought her on our trip to Hawaii—the trip that he and Mom had originally planned. I really was trying my best with Bart, and I'm sure—under the circumstances—he might have been trying to do the same with me. I understand people grieve differently. Still, no one could understand me nor did they seem to want to. "Carry on" was the only emotion I continuously picked up on from the family.

Hawaii was gorgeous. But I have to say, it would have been much more beautiful if I hadn't been minus the most important person in my life. Even in a tropical paradise, I felt lost at sea. Yet I kind of perked up when a boy I'd met invited me to go to a nude beach. Even though I was only twelve, I looked sixteen to eighteen. My body was slender, and I had thick, long brown hair and a golden tan. To look at me structurally, I looked normal, yet on the inside, I was still recovering from the accident and surgeries.

Because I was craving attention, I almost took him up on it. What stopped me? The fear of the Lord set in, and I could see Momma raising her eyebrows at me. I could hear her voice firmly shouting, "Lynz Nicole" in that same tone she'd always used to reprimand me. So I decided against going. I knew the attention I desired could only come from God. No man could satisfy my craving.

Dressed in my bikini, I ventured out on the regular beach by myself. I'd been watching people boogie board and thought it would be cool to go surfing. The sport looked easy.

While Bart was in the restaurant eating with his girlfriend, I hopped on a boogie board and headed into the water. Meanwhile, disaster struck again, but this was sort of my own fault.

I don't know how far into the ocean I'd gone. It seemed like a mile or further. What happened? My boogie board flipped out from under me, and I couldn't get my hands on it. I wasn't the most skilled swimmer, and I kept fighting against the current, but it was using up every bit of energy I had, and then some. At the same time, I was swallowing so much water I couldn't cry out for help anymore. I was literally drowning.

With not a soul around, I cried out to God with my spirit saying, "Okay. I made a stupid choice. I'm so sorry."

The governmental call upon my life—when I had the near-death experience in the accident—flashed before me. I continued pleading with the Lord. "Look! I know I have a purpose. I remember distinctly making a choice to come back. Please help me."

At that instant, this huge wave came up behind me and picked me up—the power of God is undeniable—and I rested on the wave until I hit the coral. It's like God dropped me off on a rock—

the Rock of Salvation. I got really scratched up, but that was okay. I was rescued. Then I began to vomit all the water I'd swallowed.

I climbed to the top of the rock near the shoreline. And what do you know? Along came my stepdad with his girlfriend. Nobody knew I was out there. I don't remember if he asked where I had been. I don't think he really cared. That's how life was with Bart. He'd literally left me to myself after Mom died.

CHAPTER ELEVEN

THAT WAS NOVEMBER. Fast forward to December, and I spent a few weeks with my Auntie Rose. I didn't stay consistently. During that month, I would go back and forth with my friends—just to hang out. If I could have clicked my heels—like Dorothy in *The Wizard of Oz*—and made a wish, it would be to live with Auntie Rose. She wasn't blood related, but she was the closest thing I had to a mom, and she treated me like her own daughter.

The people I wanted to live with couldn't take me in to raise so I always wound up going back to Bart's house, which wasn't what I'd call home. As difficult as it was to admit, I had become severely depressed. My losses were immense. I had no one to turn to. I wasn't offered counseling or pastoring. It seemed the little bit of family I had was of the "get over it and move on" mentality.

I had gone on a winter retreat with my youth group from church when I started looking for a butcher knife in the camp kitchen. Just because you're with church family doesn't exempt an individual from struggling. I was in one more spiritual battle. God was telling me, "Don't do it, Lynz." And Satan was pumping the poison into my head. My first step of action was to call Auntie Rose. I told her I was about to take my life with a knife, and she talked me out of committing suicide.

There was one other time when I was at home that I grabbed a butcher knife and planned to stab myself, but the presence of God was powerful enough to prevent it. I called Auntie Rose on that second attempt, too. Again, she calmed me down and told me to put the knife away. She also tried to get me help. Not having any parental rights, she could only suggest, not force anyone to get me into therapy.

So if it wasn't a car accident, a near drowning, or suicidal thoughts, I went hiking up the terrain with the people from camp and fell off the cliff. It cracked my head open, and I had to go to the hospital and have stitches—plus a shot in my head. On top of that, I still hadn't completely healed from the head injuries sustained in the car accident.

It was so crazy how I kept having head-on collisions with near-death, but I survived them all—thanks be to God.

The next adjustment I had to make is when Bart pulled me out of the private Christian school— where Mom had me enrolled—and placed me into the public school the following year. It was there that I became really close friends with a girl named Kirsty.

Kirsty was compassionate and kind. I had become very vulnerable. So when she said, "We'll be your family. We'll take care of you," that was music to my ears. Finally, someone was concerned for me. Bart didn't care where I was. I'm sure he celebrated any time I left the house because that was less time he had to deal with me. He had stopped taking me to church. I had been on and off the streets, living with different people with no stable home environment. There were no rules, no structure. I had to fend for myself.

Kirsty lived with her family in a pop-up tent/trailer on a campground. She was in a gang, and so I slicked my hair back and started dressing in all black to fit in with the company I was keeping. Also, after Mom died, I developed anorexia and bulimia. I never sought counseling to overcome it. I'd starve myself as a way to try to control a situation that was out of my control—my living conditions, my life circumstances, my insecurities of feeling unwanted and unloved. It was like this big pot of emotional stew that had been brewing quite a while without anyone noticing it was boiling over.

One day I went to the mall to hang out with Kirsty and others. We were all wearing red. Kirsty told me I was about to be jumped into a gang and gang-raped. I told her I didn't feel good about it. Truth is, there was no way I was going to be gang-raped. Intimidated by Kirsty's aggression, I told her I didn't think it was the right thing for me to do. She assured me they would be my family. This other gang happened to be at the mall at the same time, and they started throwing gang signs. That's when Kirsty started talking smack. Her sudden personality change freaked me out.

In the middle of what was about to be a gang-fight, I started saying, "The Lord bless you. The Lord keep you. God Bless you. The Lord loves you very much."

I can't say I couldn't believe what happened next because I've seen God do what man deems impossible. But the gang turned around and walked away. I was scared enough that I picked up the phone and called Bart. He might have come to pick me up, but I actually can't recall how I got home. I just know I landed back at Bart's house again.

Months after the accident, people eventually faded off, as they do. I was pretty much isolated from everyone else except Grandpa Starling. He was the last main stable staple left in my life. And I did still have my sheep—Ya Katarina—and she was amazing! I was very close to her.

When summertime came—with Grandpa Starling by my side—I did some showmanship, western pleasure, barrel racing and things like that. My horse, Feature Seven, was one highlight of my life and Grandpa Starling was the other. Both were the inspiration that kept me going... for a short while anyway.

CHAPTER TWELVE

YET AGAIN, LIFE has its ebbs and flows, its seasons of peaks and valleys. All of a sudden, my Aunt Ursula—Mom's sister—and her husband, my uncle, made arrangements with Bart—or whomever worked in the system— to take me in. I had no Guardian Ad Litem, court advocate or Child Protection Board to represent me or speak on my behalf. It was all thrust upon me with the same impact of the car that killed Mom and seriously injured me.

Word got back to me through friends that this is not what my mom would have wanted. This is not what she would ever agree to do. I found out that aside from her making comments I found strange days prior to the incident, Mom had also talked to people before the accident expressing concern for my well-being in the event something happened to her. She, obviously, had a premonition.

I remember asking, "Where am I going? What am I doing?" And they said, "You're going to go with your aunt and uncle." I asked, "Why? I don't understand."

I wasn't a bad child, but I was a broken one. And, believe me, I was in a really dark place with every reason to be. But I didn't drink, do drugs, cuss, nor was I sexually promiscuous.

Truth is Bart didn't want me. My grandmother said me living with her wouldn't work out. I couldn't stay with a girl in a gang who lived on a campground in a pop-tent/trailer. Being a minor without anyone to speak or fight on my behalf, I packed my bags.

Without any type of questioning or any type of advocating on my behalf, through the system, I was trafficked through CPS (Child Protective Services) out-of-state. For me, there was no process. No voice to be heard or represented. Absolutely nothing.

At thirteen years of age—with nothing but a suitcase full of clothes, a few pictures and Mom's Bible—I said goodbye to Arizona, the only place I'd ever called home.

Worse, I could feel the weight of evil when my aunt and uncle picked me up and flew me halfway across the country to live with them in Tennessee. The van ride from the airport to their home was not only dreadful, but it had a wicked feel about it. Like…I smelled the stench of a bad environment before I'd literally stepped inside of it, and there wasn't one darn thing I could do about it. That van had a sulfur scent, which is a sign of evil.

Not long after I'd settled in to the basement where they put me, Aunt Ursula said they'd have to get me in line, that she couldn't believe that I was dressed so inappropriately. I was still wearing all black—nothing promiscuous as she'd led me to feel—but I was in mourning. If anyone had bothered to ask, I would have told them.

I missed Auntie Rose, Grandpa Starling and my friends. But most of all, I missed my horses. Being without my animals was tough, but then Aunt Ursula started liquidating everything back in Arizona. Mom's records of things disappeared. My sheep, Ya Katarina, was sold. Mom's dog was euthanized. My cat "died."

My two-year-old Filly, Feature Seven, was red with a black mane, and she had a white star and a little white snip on her chin with three dots on her front hoof. Aunt Ursula sold Feature Seven, too. Everything good and precious in my life was being snatched away in one swoop. After all I'd been through, selling my horse nearly destroyed me.

The upside: Mom's chickens were the only living creatures saved. Her best friend took them. I always thought it was so cool that Mom had purchased a one hundred year old chicken house. That woman loved her chickens, horses, cats, dogs, and sheep. I am so grateful I inherited the animal loving gene from her.

Back to life at Aunt Ursula's: I've never been one to mind doing chores. Mom always had me clean my room and help her around the house. But my aunt was using me like a slave. I'm not talking cleaning the floor with a mop and broom. Oh, no. She had me down on my hands and knees scrubbing floors with a toothbrush. This wasn't punishment for doing anything wrong. It was common practice for them—and downright unbearable for me.

Not only was I their everyday housekeeper—doing all the laundry as well—I had become their full-time nanny, too. Not long after I was trafficked to their home, I had to get up at the crack of dawn to take care of their entire household duties, and I didn't get into bed until midnight because of the multiple chores they had me doing on top of getting my schoolwork done as well. Every single thing the parents should have been doing, I was made to do by them—leaving me no childhood of my own, just enslaved as their property.

The only clothing I had was from the suitcase I'd packed to move. Instead of buying or providing any new or decent clothes, Aunt Ursula sent me to a huge school, which was all brand new to me, wearing—of all things—her old maternity clothes. If that wasn't awkward and despicable enough, I had to wear her blood-stained underwear and her hand-me-down bras that didn't properly fit. These were her old clothes that had been locked in storage.

On the way to school, I'd get teased on the bus about those maternity clothes. Students would laugh and ask, "Are you pregnant?" I just lowered my head in shame and ignored them.

There was the question of finances. In my own mind, I couldn't help wondering what they were doing with all the money they were making from the sale of our horses and other livestock. That might explain why they cut me off from most everyone. That way I had no way to find out what they'd done or were doing with the money. Oddly enough, the one person they forced me to have a relationship with was the one person who'd caused our family so much pain—the other uncle and grandfather who had molested my momma. My grandfather was getting remarried, and I dreaded having to travel to Kansas with my aunt and uncle to visit.

When we reconnected, I asked my uncle— Mom's brother—how he could have done what he did to her. Of course, that was a touchy subject, and all he wanted to do was get away from me at breakneck speed after I hit him with that question. I was able to approach my maternal grandfather, who happened to be there as well, and I asked him the same. His answer, "Well, I repented for what I did."

Good for him. I pray he did ask for the Lord's forgiveness because he certainly needed to.

CHAPTER THIRTEEN

I WAS STILL SUFFERING anorexia. Bulimia followed. I started forcing myself to vomit after I would eat. I wasn't happy doing that, and I wanted to stop. I'll always believe every bit of grief I had suffered was cooking internally. Then I was regurgitating it out—an unhealthy way of ridding myself from the pain. That condition became a form of my own coping mechanism.

As if I hadn't already been through enough, my uncle—Aunt Ursula's husband—started exposing himself to me. And I just threw my head back in utter disgust and asked myself a question I couldn't begin to answer. *What in the world did I end up here for? Like…you've got to be kidding me.*

It might sound unbelievable that my life was like a mountain of boulders crashing down in succession, but it is nothing but the honest to God's truth. It's the kind of stuff an award winning novelist can't even begin to imagine. I, myself, was hardly able to believe it was all occurring. I just needed for it to stop.

But it didn't end with the exposure…sorry to say. My uncle started coming down into the basement when I was sleeping. When he crawled into my bed and began groping me—feeling me from one end of my body to the other—I froze. I mean, I cringed actually. His sexual assaults against me began.

Then he would get up, shower, get dressed and go to work. This always happened when Aunt Ursula wasn't home. The minute she would back out of the driveway and head to work, he'd come downstairs and crawl on top of me and start his sick and psycho nastiness all over again. Whenever my aunt left the house to go anywhere, I became frightened out of my mind because I knew what her husband was going to do.

Every single time he threw himself on top of me, I wanted to run out of the house screaming, but I was too afraid of the repercussions. What would happen if I squealed? Would I turn up missing to later be found buried in a shallow grave? Those are the thoughts that always crossed my mind. Eventually, he stole the one thing I could never get back: my innocence.

Long story short: There wasn't a day that went by that I didn't have to deal with my uncle raping me. It was always against my will, but he tried to convince me that it was my fault and that I was seducing him. And that couldn't have been further from the truth.

We traveled back to Arizona, but it wasn't to return me to my roots. They wanted to adopt me and had to take me back home for the legal process. I didn't want any part of that family or name, and I told them not to follow through with it. I asked if that would mean forever removing Mom's name from my birth certificate. They told me it would. And I said, "No. I don't want that."

Never mind what my wishes were. I told the judge what they wanted to hear because I was terrified of them. They were evil and violent. They not only screamed at me, they screamed at their kids, too. I would wrap my legs around the legs of the dining room table—thinking it was a safe place—as I shuddered in horror while they beat the crap out of each of them with a belt or whatever they could get their hands on to use as a weapon for punishment.

I was mortified—not to mention my uncle was a pervert, sexually assaulting me, proudly displaying his privates as if they were a trophy. But I dare not tell that or I might become a statistic. Back to Tennessee I went—this time with a different last name I didn't want.

CHAPTER FOURTEEN

I LEARNED AS A teenager that not everyone who attends church truly walks with the Lord. The lifestyle I knew about in private and the wonderful worshipping persona my aunt and my uncle exhibited in public sickened me. Aunt Ursula was as mean as my uncle was perverted. But their evil didn't stop them from gracing the doors of the Baptist Church as if they believed themselves to be saints. Members of the congregation had no idea of the horrors happening inside of that house. I shudder when I think back on all the dysfunction and evil.

But God blessed me, though it was through the sinister couple walking in darkness who drove me to church. At First Baptist, I met a good Christian guy and later became his girlfriend. Let me tell you…he was the sweetest, kindest, most compassionate young man I'd ever known besides Grandpa Starling. I never slept with him. In fact, we barely even kissed or held hands. I was able to confide in him about all the disturbing activity taking place behind closed doors at Aunt Ursula's.

He listened without judgment and consoled me every time I needed to vent. He expected nothing in return nor did he try to force his way with me. I'll never forget how understanding he was, and it was a gift to have been introduced to such a sweetheart of a guy after having seen the worst side of men via male members in my own family.

We—myself and their biological children—were constantly in trouble for something stupid that didn't warrant being grounded. It was constant. So any time I could escape the confines of the "House of Horrors," I would. If a friend invited me over, I would spend the night to avoid being sexually assaulted by my uncle. When other couples needed a babysitter, I volunteered—anything to get me away from Aunt Ursula and my twisted uncle.

When I obtained a driving permit, my uncle would ride along because, by law, a licensed driver had to be present. I was so afraid to get behind the wheel with him in the car because he couldn't keep his hands off me. While I was trying to focus on the road, he touched and grabbed me in my genital areas. I would jump. One time, I almost ran into a ditch because I became so irritated, distracted, and consumed with fear.

My uncle, through marriage, was the horniest, most sexually perverted, distorted and obscene man I'd ever known—and fifteen years my senior. The older I got, the stronger my rage and resentment toward him became. I thought about my mother. God rest her sweet and gentle soul. She'd tried everything within her power to protect me and to prevent what had happened to her from happening to me.

There was one instance where I was on the couch, and he was going to start that number of his with me. I got up, and he chased me around the wraparound that was near the kitchen/garage area of the home. I was hoping to escape that time, but he eventually caught me, threw me on the sofa and got on top of me. What would make a man—a married one at that—sexually assault a child? Nothing but a depraved mind and pure evil. I couldn't have been more disgusted. I would try to push him away and scream at him to get off of me, but he continued forcing himself on me.

At school, I overheard people making comments about the clothing I had to wear—the maternity dresses and blood-stained undergarments they'd see when I dressed out for physical education class. I was so embarrassed. But I could not explain to them my wardrobe was handpicked by *Cruella Deville*—Aunt Ursula—and her selection was the equivalent to what you might find at the city dump.

If I wasn't catching heat at school for the pitiable clothes I was dressed in, I'd come home to my uncle's sexual innuendos, crude comments and— worse—being repeatedly raped.

When I was a sophomore in high school, I found out you could become emancipated at sixteen in the state of Tennessee if you could find a job and a place to live to take care of yourself so you could be self-sustaining. I started desperately trying to find a way to get out of that house.

Unlucky for me, my uncle had started working from home, and he set his office up in the basement where my bedroom happened to be. Even though my aunt never said a word about what my uncle was doing to me, I know she had to know.

Early one morning, I was asleep in my bed. My aunt had gone to work. I woke up to him touching and kissing me, and I started shaking. The rape process was a repetitive pattern. I lost track of the number of times, but I had reached my limit with that nearly three hundred pound tub of lard plopping himself on top of me.

This supernatural strength came over me. I shot out of the bed, shoved him, and he flew off of me. Then I shouted, "I say in the fear of the Lord, you have to stop. I'm not going to do this anymore. You have to tell Aunt Ursula. And if you don't, I will."

I got dressed and went to school that day. But that evening, my aunt and uncle came into my room. And staring straight through me with those monster-looking eyeballs, she said, "If you ever say anything to anyone, we will deny it. We will tell them you're lying."

And I pleaded with her, "But this is what's happening to me. You have to do something. I'm not going to do this anymore."

Aunt Ursula showed not one bit of sympathy, empathy or even a smidgen of willingness to try and understand.

With the two of them against one of me, I felt my safety was at risk. I was so nervous, I can't recall every single thing they said, but I do remember fearing for my life because of how angry and violent I'd seen them get in the home and with me that night.

Realizing Aunt Ursula wasn't going to do one thing about it and was actually threatening me if I told, I made my plans.

CHAPTER FIFTEEN

THE FOLLOWING MORNING, I packed
Mom's Bible—along with the wretched,
maternity clothes I'd been wearing—inside a
little gym bag before I caught the bus. When I
arrived at school, the first thing I did was put a
note on my counselor's door that I needed to talk
with her.

Mrs. Burke, my favorite teacher, taught science.
By the time I got to her class, I couldn't function.
I know I had a gym bag, Mom's Bible, textbooks,
writing instruments and lessons I was working
on; but, honestly, I couldn't focus in class for
worrying about what the outcome would be for
ratting on my uncle. Aunt Ursula clearly sided
with him and wasn't going to help me out. Her
defending him didn't astound me. Partners in
crime—the two of them.

It was getting near the end of the school day, and
I hadn't heard back from the counselor. Engulfed
by fear, I had to talk to somebody. There was no
way I was going home. I had this horrible feeling
that something bad was going to happen to me
if I did.

I did the best I could to try to suppress my emotions, but I felt this massive meltdown coming on. I didn't want to have a major waterworks show in front of anyone, especially the classmates who'd already poked fun at my clothing. So I told Mrs. Burke I needed to step outside the classroom.

Once I got into the hallway, I sat down and began crying uncontrollably. I think tears sprung from every bit of trauma I'd endured since the accident that took the life of Momma. That wailing cry I never really got to have occurred in the school hall, and I was a complete wreck.

My friend, Tiffany, came and sat outside in the hall with me. With an overwhelming sense of sympathy, she asked, "What's wrong? What's going on?"

In between choking back tears, I said, "I've got to talk to the school counselor."

I'm pretty sure Mrs. Burke knew something was terribly wrong. At that point, the counselor actually announced my name over the intercom and called me into the office. Mrs. Burke granted me permission to go speak with the counselor.

I walked into her office, looked her square in the face and mustered the courage to say, "I know that what I'm going to tell you…you'll have to call the police. I can't go home. I fear for my life." And I proceeded to tell her about my uncle sexually assaulting me for the past three and a half years. I added, "He needs to be arrested. I can't do this anymore."

The police were called to the school. Shortly thereafter, Aunt Ursula showed up. Law enforcement officers interviewed me on VHS tape, and they also interviewed my aunt. I can't exactly recall, but I think she admitted to it on tape.

Because I was sixteen and considered age of consent, they basically told me there had to be a temporary place that I could go until they could find a place to put me. I had no advocate, no Guardian Ad Litem, no one taking me to the hospital to have me checked out. Nothing.

When the officers approached me and said, "You have to ride in the car with her," I was taken aback. The last place I wanted to be was locked up inside a car with Aunt Ursula. I told them, "You don't understand."

Before I could finish explaining why I didn't want to ride with her, they assured me, "We will be escorting you. We will be right behind you. It will be okay. She has been instructed that she cannot say one word to you in the car."

They held their promise! I felt safe with the police following closely behind us. But my aunt violated the officers' orders when she asked me,

"Why did you do this? We could have worked this out."

And I quickly reminded her, "No. I asked you for help, and you didn't do a thing. Mom would be so disappointed in you." She didn't say another word after that.

The kindest thing my aunt ever did for me was to drive me to her best friend Lynn's house, where she dropped me off. I got out of her car carrying my little gym bag, still toting Mom's Bible around in it. Lord knows I needed it with me at all times. Before Aunt Ursula drove away, she talked to Lynn outside for a few minutes. The police were still present. They waited for me to go inside the house and for my aunt to leave the premises.

Lynn was great! She never talked about what happened or why I was at her house. In fact, she said, "I've been instructed not to talk to you about this." She also told me she didn't want to get into the middle of it because Aunt Ursula was her best friend. She treated me with the utmost kindness and respect. And when she saw my clothes, she took me to The Limited and to Express and bought me a whole new wardrobe. I had brand new underwear, bras, and the most adorable outfits—a complete switch from my previous wardrobe.

I only stayed with Lynn for three days, but those were the best three days I could remember since before Mom had died.

Next—and I don't even know how it happened—I wound up staying with one of my best friends' for two to three weeks. There wasn't even a bed for me, but I didn't mind sleeping on the floor. I would have been satisfied sleeping on the ground outside during a deep freeze as long as it kept me away from my perverted uncle.

The problem that arose at my friend's house is that she was getting asked questions all over school about what happened. Her mother was a single mom, and I can understand why they didn't want any involvement with my drama. She let me stay a little while longer—until I could find a place to go—but I knew I would eventually have to leave.

The District Attorney's office was pressing charges against my uncle. I was scrambling to find space and place—anywhere to not have to go back to the "House of Horrors." Meanwhile, I was left to my own again…kind of like I had been at Bart's before being bused off to Tennessee.

My uncle was arrested, but then he bailed out. I couldn't, obviously, go back. My aunt remained married to him.

I got on the computer—this is when it was still Internet dial-up service—and I made contact with someone from my past who I could only hope would be willing to take me in and help me out until I could get on my feet.

I dialed the number; a man answered. I asked, "Is this John Clark?"

He said, "Yes."

My next question, "Did you used to have a daughter named Lynz?"

He said, "Yes."

Feeling like this was my last hope, I told my real dad that I was his daughter, and I explained everything that had happened to me.

CHAPTER SIXTEEN

I CAN'T TELL YOU how elated I was and how free I felt when the plane I'd boarded landed on the tarmac in Utah—the place of my birth. My dad, who hadn't raised me and whom I really didn't know, rescued me! I am thankful every day that he was not only sympathetic, but truly mad and hurt at how I'd been abused at the hands of my uncle.

After having no contact with him for years, I found out my paternal grandparents were divorced, and they had each remarried. When my flight landed in Utah, my paternal grandmother and step-grandad picked me up at the airport. They were amazing people.

My father and stepmom were truck drivers. With them being on the road so often, I actually lived with my paternal grandparents for a couple of years.

Even though my paternal grandparents had divorced and remarried other people, both couples got along really well—like best friends— and that kind of behavior was unfamiliar to me. I found it to be so unique and fun!

Initially, when I first reconnected with my biological father, everything seemed fine. We got along well. Being out of the hell home in Tennessee was like catching a deep breath after being depleted of good oxygen for so long. But Dad told me he had a lot of reprogramming to do because he said my mom had screwed up on the raising.

Needless to say, I took offense to his remark, and I took up for her. "My mom is not here to defend herself. I don't know what happened between the two of y'all, but she was a damn good mother, and you won't speak ill about her ever again."

After having been locked up in the "House of Horrors" having no voice and no choice to say or do anything for so many years, I was becoming a fighter and a defender without fully grasping the depth of my strength at times.

I did get along with John Clark, my biological father, but we had our ups and downs. One of them was that he had been in touch with the District Attorney's office in Tennessee. And when it came time for me to return for the sexual assault case, my father did everything within his power to talk me out of testifying and tried to convince me to let my uncle take a plea bargain. After I'd suffered three long years at the hands of that creep, I wanted him to spend time in jail and have to pay for what he'd done. He needed to experience what being locked up felt like—get a good dose of his own medicine.

My father's reasoning didn't make any sense to me. It only made me mad when he said, "You just don't need to go through that."

So I let my father win that battle by allowing my uncle to plea bargain. The pervert didn't get much more than a slap on the hand. Because I was a teenager, I was certain he'd at least have to register as a sex offender. But he got off scot free on that front, too. "Pay a little fine to avoid the time," is what I've always said.

CHAPTER SEVENTEEN

I TRIED TO HAVE a relationship with my dad—a healthy one like many of my friends seemed to have with their fathers. In my eyes, he could do no wrong. Then again, throughout my whole life, I didn't really know him. I loved that he was a cowboy; however, I didn't like that he drank more than I would have liked for him to.

On the other hand, I'd developed a zero tolerance to bull crap after spending all that time enslaved. There were things I just couldn't and wouldn't put up with. Basically, we had a "Yo-Yo" relationship—up and down. Then again, maybe I was looking for perfection from my father when what I really needed was tenderness and affection. Unlike my life in Tennessee where I did nothing but scrub the floors with a toothbrush, feed babies, change diapers, get bullied at school and assaulted at home, I was happy and productive living with my grandparents in Utah.

During my junior year of high school, I took a first responder's course. My senior year, I ran as an EMT. Not everyone is cut out for that job. But having had my encounter with death in a car accident that killed my mom, I could handle the unpleasant sights and scenes we came upon. Helping people became a passion.

In December 2000, which was my senior year of high school, I met a guy two years older than me and fell head over heels in love. Just like my dad, he was a cowboy! Within a few months, we became engaged. I remembered I'd always told Momma I'd marry a cowboy or an Air Force Cadet.

Much to my dismay, my father and his family saw the handwriting on the wall and tried to direct my attention to it, but I refused to even look. Sometimes people have to discover the truth for themselves even when others clearly see and point it out. Such was the case with my marriage. They tried to talk me out of tying the knot, but I followed through with the wedding. My biological father gave me away, even though he wasn't in favor of who I was marrying.

After four years of being in an abusive relationship, we divorced. The one and only good thing that came from that marriage was my first born daughter—well, plus a major life lesson learned. It's easy to get married, but getting divorced is difficult.

I was fortunate enough to obtain a realtor's license, and I started selling properties. At the same time I was working to support myself, I was in a custody battle with my ex-husband, and it was wreaking havoc between me and my dad. He used to say that if my marriage didn't work out, that he would keep my ex-husband and get rid of me. Although he was joking, he did follow through on that.

Eventually, I got my daughter back, but not without a bloodbath of a court fight.

CHAPTER EIGHTEEN

FROM A BAD situation, life birthed something beautiful—another gift from God—yet there was a strange twist in the way the Lord delivered it. Isn't that always the case? Nothing is as ever as we expect it. What helped it happen? I'm so much like my mom, wherein I can talk to anybody, anywhere, anytime about most anything.

In 2005, my daughter had fallen very ill and was admitted to the hospital. The respiratory therapist's name was Lorelei, and we had shared some intimate conversations. She knew I was a single mom.

One day she said to me, "You need to get out, and you need to do something. You need to meet someone."

All I wanted at that point was for my daughter to get well so we could vacate that hospital. The last thing on my mind was traipsing onto the dating field to try and find a boyfriend or another husband, especially after going through the process of a divorce.

I will never forget my reply: "I don't need or want another man. I'm good. I just want to raise my daughter and be on my own."

So for a very short duration, Lorelei persisted with trying to hook me up, introducing me to what seemed every available man in the city, state, and country. I have to hand it to her...she really did know a lot of single guys.

What wound up happening is I caved to the pressure and let Lorelei set me up with some different men. Nothing worked out with any of them. Besides that, I always put my daughter first. Lorelei kept insisting on introducing me to more of her male friends. Finally, I said, "No more." She was so determined to find a good and decent partner for me, and I appreciated her effort. But dating can be exhausting.

When Lorelei said, "Well, there is one more I want to introduce you to," I just threw my head back in disgust. Again, I said, "I'm done. You've introduced me to so many people. I'm tired. I feel like I'm speed dating. Seriously, I mean it...I'm done."

But then she added something that piqued my interest. "Well," she told me, "he is in the Air Force."

Turns out, her first husband had single male friends he'd served with in the military.

And I asked her to show me a picture of him. She did. And I remember commenting, "He is really handsome." There was something about him, too. Maybe it was his smile.

In my mind, I was thinking he was stationed at a nearby base, just a few hours away. But then she informed me that he was stationed in North Dakota.

I asked, "So you're trying to hook me up with a guy that's stationed in North Dakota?"

And she said, "No. Actually, he's not there right now. He's deployed overseas."

At this point, I just laughed and twisted her statement into a question. "So now you're trying to set me up with a guy that's not even stateside?" And then I quizzed her on why she was trying to set me up with a man several states away from where I was in Utah. To me, that made no sense. It wasn't practical for him or for me.

But Lorelei seemed to have this blind confidence about us and actually said, "I think you would be great together. I think you two would get married."

I shot her a look and said, "You're crazy." I'm not being snarky at all. I speak about Lorelei in kind because she cared so much about me and my daughter. All she wanted was the best for us.

So she invited me to her home and she sat me down at her computer and said, "Just email him from my email. And if he's still interested, you just never know what can happen."

Thinking it was the dumbest idea ever, I emailed the guy—more for Lorelei than for me. Everything that would cause a man to hightail it in the opposite direction is exactly what I wrote, which was nothing but the absolute truth.

Here it goes: "I'm a single mom. Basically, I'm high maintenance. If you're not a Christian, I don't want anything to do with you. I don't know if I can have any more kids. I'm in bankruptcy. I get my hair and nails done once a week. I don't want your support. I work out all the time. And I don't need a man. So if you're still interested in me, email me back."

There wasn't a doubt in my mind that I ended a relationship with him before it could begin. But, no, I thought I would need shock paddles to restore my heart rhythm when he actually emailed me back. His name: Jeremy. Believe it or not, we became pen pals. We would speak hours a day through Yahoo chat and via different online messaging systems.

Meanwhile, I had returned to my job in the medical field, and my daughter had recovered. Praise Jesus!

Herein comes a real shocker. After getting to know one another through countless and enchanting emails and online chats wherein we related on all personal, mental, spiritual, emotional and professional levels, Jeremy proposed through Yahoo Messenger.

I thought he was joking so I played along. "Sure. Whatever. Let's do it," I said.

Then one day while I was working the medical field, my co-workers said, "There is a Jeremy on the line that said he needs to speak with you.

I was sort of stunned and I told them, "I don't know a Jeremy."

With that, they hung up on him. He called right back. And, again, they said, "It's Jeremy. Your fiancé? You're engaged?" they surprisingly asked.

Then it hit me, and I replied, "Well, I guess I am." Silly me for being so absentminded. I just didn't expect him to call me at the office. When he did, I was brainstorming for any guys I knew locally who were named Jeremy, not my fiancé, who I was certain was kidding when he proposed.

By the way, he was calling my office on the satellite phone, which is really expensive, so that impressed the heck out of me that he would spend that kind of money to try to reach me.

When I got on the line with him, he asked, "Are we still getting married?"

I said, "Sure! Why not?"

Jeremy had never laid eyes on me, yet I had snail-mailed a picture of me and my daughter, but he hadn't received it. He proposed—literally—sight unseen. We had fallen in love with each other's personalities plus our spirits just resonated.

I moved into his house before I ever met him in person. He was still deployed overseas and wasn't even there. Talk about crazy! I was just that certain about Jeremy. What happened next?

CHAPTER NINETEEN

I WAS WORKING SEVERAL jobs to make ends meet. I didn't have health insurance, and I became gravely ill and was running a fever. From being an EMT, I knew the signs of an infection. To get checked out, I was going to a clinic that would accept patients who didn't have insurance. On each and every visit, they said, "There is nothing wrong. Just take Ibuprofen and Tylenol, and you'll be fine."

I know my own body, and I knew I wasn't "fine" as they'd tried to convince me. I felt a lump on the anterior side of my left breast. It got to the point where I woke up one day with red streaks on that area.

But I was addicted to jogging, and not much would keep me from heading out for a run— not even an infection. I was still suffering from eating disorders so if I ate a cookie or anything unhealthy, I would jog until I'd burned the amount of calories I had consumed.

So as bad as I felt that day, I still took off for a two and a half mile jog with a friend. And that's when things went really south. I felt something sloshing around. Not to get too graphic, but I pulled my shirt open, and it literally ripped the skin off my breast. Puss and fluid poured out. It was not only a grotesque sight but extremely frightening.

My jogging buddy saw it with her own eyes and rushed me to the ER. I was met by Dr. Tunde, who examined me. He asked me why I'd waited so long, and I explained that I had been to the clinic two or three times already and they hadn't done a thorough exam—just sent me home with instructions to take anti-inflammatories.

He said, "I have to take you into surgery right now."

And I asked, "Why?"

He expressed, "This is a big deal."

He dashed me through to emergency surgery, cut open my left breast, and had to debride it and clean out everything. He had to use a vacuum pump, which creates negative pressure around the wound and pulls the edges of the wound together—a wound vac packed with surgical mesh substance.

It was one thing after another. During that ordeal, I tested positive for MRSA—staph infection. I felt like actress Lucille Wall in a medical debacle episode of *Portia Faces Life*—only my debacles were being played out in real-life, not on a television soap opera.

There I was engaged to Jeremy. In the next instant, I was rushed through emergency surgery and then diagnosed with methicillin-resistant staphylococcus aureus.

The good news is—thanks to God and Dr. Tunde—I recovered. In fact, Dr. Tunde saved my life in more ways than one. After the surgery and staph, he said, "I'm going to give you medication. It is eight hundred dollars a pill. Make sure you take it."

If only every physician could be as kind and caring as Dr. Tunde. He knew I had no insurance so he *gave* me the eight hundred dollar medication, which helped me heal. As unfortunate as my health scare was, I wound up not having to pay a dime for the surgery because the clinic misdiagnosed it.

CHAPTER TWENTY

ALONG CAME MY birthday—September 13th—and what a surprise it was. Jeremy flew into town. I met him in person for the first time. We kissed…for the first time!

Three days later, we got married before a Justice of the Peace on the 16th of September in the year 2005. Our friends stood in for us. It was a most unusual but awesome experience. When you know, you know. Jeremy Loomis was meant for me.

I was much better but not fully recovered, and he took care of me. This incredible man took me just the way I was. And then I almost accidentally killed him. I had learned to cook a little better in my twenties than in my tweens and teens, so I prepared a dish Momma used to make called King Ranch Chicken.

Having only been married a few days—and without ever dating him—I didn't know Jeremy's food sensitivities. Come to find out, he was allergic to almost every ingredient I'd put in the chicken. He was saying, "I can't eat this, and I can't eat that."

The King Ranch Chicken I'd prepared was loaded with onions and bell peppers—a few of the herbs and spices he said he had major intolerances to. Honestly, I wondered if he was really allergic to certain foods or if that was his polite way of telling me the dish wasn't fit to eat. When I tasted it, I said, "It doesn't taste like Mom's."

We scooted our chairs back from the table, got up and went to Applebee's to eat and to celebrate as that was actually our first official date. In memory of my epic fail with the King Ranch Chicken, Jeremy and I have made it a fun tradition to commemorate our anniversary every year at Applebee's.

After dinner that night, we returned home and dove into the cream cheese pie I'd made for his birthday, which was September 6th—the week prior to mine. September is our month with both our birthdays and an anniversary to celebrate! Not to brag, but I did manage to knock the dessert out of the park for him, so that redeemed Jeremy's trust in my cooking capabilities. But that wouldn't last long!

I was taken aback, though, when Jeremy said to me, "We need a church wedding."

I asked him, "Why?" He explained that his grandmother really wanted us to have a church wedding. His grandparents pretty much raised him. Being incredibly close with them his whole life, he wanted to honor their wishes and marry in traditional fashion.

I didn't really want a church wedding, but I knew it was important to Jeremy and his grandparents, who were absolutely precious. We tried to get the wedding on my Mom's birthday—December 10th—but the chapel wasn't open because it was so close to Christmas. To have been able to marry on Mom's birthday would have been so special, but we were only one day off.

On Friday evening, December 9th, Jeremy and I exchanged vows—again—but this time inside a church sanctuary at the Air Force base chapel. I'm so glad we followed through with his grandparents' request.

Of course, nothing is ever normal with us, which makes life all the more fun and interesting. All of Jeremy's Air Force Squadron were in an exercise so guests had to take shifts coming to the ceremony. It cracked me up with his Air Force buddies entering and exiting during our wedding.

Super cool is we had the Honor Guard present. Wedding tradition worldwide is when you marry someone in the Air Force, sabers or swords are used to salute a newly married couple. The bride and groom pass under an honorary arch of sabers when exiting the church or the building where the wedding was held, and the last sword the couple walks passed smacks the bride on the behind—but not very hard. I felt a little pop, which reminded me of Momma and that infamous wooden spoon.

I did not end up marrying an Air Force *Cadet* as I had told my mother as a child. Instead, I married the best Airman. For the past sixteen years—and until the end of time—I'll forever remain married to Jeremy Loomis, *my* Air Force Airman and hero!

My hat is off to Lorelei! I owe her a lifetime of gratitude. She was so persistent pushing me to get out there and date. When she said she thought Jeremy and I would marry, she was spot on!

CHAPTER TWENTY-ONE

SEASONS ARRIVE WHEN we finally get what we want. It's always wonderful when everything perfectly falls into place. But is it ever enough? I'm sure everyone can relate. Those times come when—well, we have another hurdle to jump.

When I married Jeremy on September 16th, 2005, he was an NCO (non-commissioned officer), and it was nicely welcomed that I would be a part of his career and that I could get involved as a key spouse. For instance, if someone in the home was pregnant and her husband was deployed, her yard was taken care of by the spouse's squadron. If someone died and the spouse needed to be notified, the military would come in as aid and comfort and fill in. If there were events of keeping and building community, the NCO member's wife was usually the point of contact, and the commander's wife was actually the one in charge. Although, I wasn't upper anything, I enjoyed serving as a key spouse.

Because the Air Force has what they refer to as "TDY's, which is an abbreviation for "Temporary Duty Orders," he really encouraged my role as a key spouse and getting to know more people.

Air Force deployments can range from four to six months. They can stretch longer, but that's usually to places like the Middle East. If they are deployed to Korea, the time away from home could be a year or longer.

Even though his base was North Dakota, he went on TDY's frequently throughout his career as well as multiple deployments.

My oldest daughter was three years old at the time, and I wasn't ready to have another child just yet. But on a routine appointment, my doctor said, "If you're going to have any more children, you need to do it sooner rather than later."

I had wanted to wait five years before having another baby. But when the doctor encouraged me to not hold off too long trying, it started me thinking.

At the beginning of 2006, I changed my mind. Go figure. And then I couldn't get pregnant. We tried so many times, I gave up hope. Because I'd had so many issues from surgeries from the accident and from the sexual assault trauma, I'm fortunate to have become pregnant and given birth to my oldest.

So when I couldn't conceive, I decided to go back on the pill. A lot of weekends, we'd go camping with our military friends. Then Jeremy volunteered for deployment to make extra money, but he hadn't left yet. It was funny because I was a size two, and I could see and feel a bump and was certain I was pregnant. I had told my husband I thought I might be pregnant, but he dismissed the idea.

Six days before Jeremy was deploying, I went to the store and bought almost every single brand and type of pregnancy tests on the market. I went home and urinated on all these different pregnancy tests. And wouldn't you know? Every single one of them was positive. Up until that point, all the tests had been negative.

I was beside myself with glee, and I started screaming with excitement. I couldn't wait to show Jeremy. When I stuck the positive pregnancy tests in his face, I said "See! I told you."

Then it dawned on me he was leaving and I had a little freak-out moment. I had found out that I was near my second trimester—ten weeks pregnant.

"I am high risk due to blood clots," I told him. "So you cannot deploy. You immediately have to cancel." I cautioned and pleaded with him at the same time.

Jeremy said, "I can't cancel."

Disappointed—and trying to drive the message home—I repeated, "But I'm high risk."

Every time I reflect back to that time, I hear the lyrics to the Beatles song, "You can't always get what you want."

Jeremy deployed.

I went to a high risk pregnancy doctor by myself. He performed an ultrasound. Sure enough, he confirmed I was expecting, and I was almost in my second trimester.

Jeremy was off in God-knows-where, and I went to the ER bleeding. I couldn't believe the nerve of this doctor. There I was laid up in a hospital bed frightened I was about to lose my baby, and this physician addressed my bleeding as if it was a mild papercut. "Well, if you're going to miscarry, you're going to miscarry," he nonchalantly stated. Not only was his comment crass, but he looked and reminded me of a pedophile. And I'd had my experience with predators so I immediately fired him and got a different doctor whose name was Dr. Ari Fishbach. I called him Dr. Fish, and he was phenomenal. I'd give him five stars plus in all areas of care. He put me on progesterone shots and he ordered me to be on bedrest.

I had been working full-time—actually over forty hours a week—at a law office.

And, too, at that time we had a couple living with us, who annoyed me to no end. I had taken a second job at Wal-Mart just to avoid being in their company. But after having been ordered on bedrest, I was stuck at home with them.

They smoked like ashtrays. I posted "No Smoking" signs throughout my home. That didn't stop them. Then I took pictures of my oldest child and my unborn baby and hung homemade signs around the house that read, "You are killing me." Those two still lit up as if they'd die if they didn't take a drag off their cigarettes every thirty minutes. My glaring stare at them made angry look like a sweet disposition to have. They weren't contributing a dime toward the bills, and I'd had it.

We had a four hundred dollar gas bill one month, not abnormal for a winter in North Dakota. I needed a baby crib and couldn't afford a new one so I had to settle for a broken-down crib—I mean, like from the 1960s or 1970s. And I was so disappointed my newborn wouldn't have a decent crib to come home to.

With me unable to work and having that couple take advantage of us financially, I couldn't deal with it anymore.

I sent a message via email to Jeremy overseas, which read, "I'm moving out. I'm not leaving you, but they won't stop smoking. They are mooching off of us, and if they won't get out, I have to temporarily separate myself from the stress and harm they could be causing me, our oldest, and our unborn child with their constant smoking."

Good grief, we'd almost had our car repossessed because of the financial burdens they were causing us but—through help from our military friends—I made arrangements to prevent that from happening. We were blessed to have one car almost paid for in the event the other had been taken from us.

At that point, I was every negative emotion wrapped inside of one: bitter, angry, madder than a hornet because everything was supposed to be peachy keen, and it wasn't.

To this day, I still don't know what Jeremy said to the couple, but they knew they'd have to get out. They had sucked up all of my air. And there they were living in my home doing absolutely nothing. I got far more help from the military than I did from them. I didn't have to worry about the yard or the snow blowing. I love that the military takes care of military.

When Jeremy left, I had a little bump. By the time he returned home from being deployed, I was almost ready to deliver. My frustrations from everything I had dealt with on my own melted when I greeted my husband as he stepped off the plane before he went to his debriefing.

As thrilled as we were to see each other, Jeremy was hurting so badly because Michael, one of his troops, was killed. And losing a comrade is emotional torture. It ripped me up to see Jeremy so distraught. All I could do to console was throw my arms around him and hold him. He was suicidal, which was one of the scariest moments of our marriage. I told him I would go to his commander and get him help if he wouldn't go. But he was able to get help. And in the process, he was also working to rid our home of the freeloaders. I can't explain how refreshing it was to know they would be vacating…like I could breathe deep for the first time in a long while.

On a Sunday, I was literally helping the spongers move out of my house and into a place of their own when I was pulled over for a speeding ticket. I told the police officer my water had broken, and I'm forever grateful he let me go without writing a ticket. I wasn't lying. My water had broken the day before, but it was a trickle, not enough to send me into delivery.

However, after being in labor forty-three hours later, I gave birth to our youngest daughter the next day—on Monday evening, March 12th, 2007. A short while later—after I'd healed from delivering my second child—I had a partial hysterectomy.

Being high risk and uncertain if I could get pregnant a second time, I am so grateful to God for my two daughters.

As a side note: Jeremy vows our youngest was conceived on July 4th, 2006. I wouldn't doubt him for a minute. With both of us being lovers of country and freedom fighters, it would be just like God to ordain America's birthday as the date our youngest daughter began to form in my womb.

CHAPTER TWENTY-TWO

I CANNOT LIE. MY journey with my husband has been very hard. Two years into our marriage—and even as happy newlyweds—we had our ups and downs. I became greatly concerned when Jeremy's migraines worsened. He had sustained multiple TBI's (traumatic brain injuries) over the course of his military career—two significant ones.

I took him to a neurologist. They did a scan, and we found out how bad it was.

When our daughter was born, Jeremy couldn't hold her for the first twenty-four hours because he had undergone a body scan with radioactive dye. The doctors were trying to find out why my hero was presenting with symptoms of Alzheimer Disease. We would later learn that the symptoms were a direct result of the multiple traumatic brain injuries he had sustained.

While on active duty in the Air Force, Jeremy suffered severe injuries to his head, neck, and back while serving in combat zones in Kuwait and in Saudi Arabia. His doctor said there was a medication he could try, but he didn't have confidence it would work.

Diamox was the recommended medicine designed to reduce the fluid in the body, reduce seizures and help with altitude sickness. Jeremy opted to try the Diamox first because he was trying to avoid the surgery. He didn't want to get kicked out of the military and labeled what we had coined a "government throwaway."

Imagine, if you will, a military member who had dedicated a life of service to their country and then being kicked to the curb by the government for injuries sustained in battle. The mere thought was disheartening—to put it mildly—and completely unfathomable to put it cruelly.

We'd just gotten back from a trip, and Jeremy wasn't feeling good so I dropped him off at the house, and I went to Wendy's and got him some food. When I returned home, he tried to stand up and his gait was wobbly. He could speak coherently, but I looked at his pupils and they were not as reactive. They looked extremely weird. From my experience working in the medical field, I knew this indicated an underlying issue.

Because of Jeremy's frequent doctors' visits, I had the neurosurgeon's phone number. I grabbed my cell, called him and said, "I am rushing my husband to the hospital. I think he is hemorrhaging."

Jeremy would not let me call an ambulance. He was able to articulate that before his speech became funky. He wasn't combative like in an aggressive way, but he was grumpy. I knew something was dangerously wrong. He started trailing off while trying to speak, and then he lost the ability to communicate what was going on. I feared he was hemorrhaging. I managed to get him to the car, and I rushed him to the hospital. The neurosurgeon was there waiting. All of this happened within seconds. It was a small town so it didn't take me long to get from our home to the hospital.

His neurosurgeon examined Jeremy and informed me, "If I don't take him in for surgery, he's going to die. I recommend airlifting him because of the type of surgery but he will not survive the trip." I was so conflicted because his doctor recommended airlifting him to a more suitable facility. He said he felt he could make it if he did. Then he added, "But either way, there is a fifty/ fifty shot of survival."

It was a small hospital with a limited trauma center. Time was of the essence, and I wasn't sure he would survive the wait to be airlifted so I gave the neurosurgeon the green light to operate on Jeremy.

Before the surgery, I called the pastor and requested prayer. On the preacher's way to the hospital, he nearly got into a wreck. Praise God, he avoided the accident and arrived in time to pray over Jeremy. Spiritual warfare is so real.

Right before I made the decision, God dropped it into my spirit and said, "You need to tell Jeremy he's going to be given a chance to go over or stay, and he needs to stay because I am not through with him yet."

For a moment, Jeremy became lucid. I prefaced what God placed into my spirit when I said, "This is our only option. You have to fight. You have to come back."

It made me well up when I saw tears in my husband's eyes. At that moment, I kissed him goodbye, and I told him I loved him as I watched the medical staff wheel him back into the operating room. I was told the surgery would take hours, and that they would put in at least two shunts, maybe even a third shunt—the ventricular shunt to help with the fluid in the brain.

The multiple head injuries created this condition where the ventricles in the brain stayed open and lost their elasticity for the production of spinal fluid.

His Air Force commander came in and was praying for me. Within a half hour, word had spread around the base, and I was surrounded by my military family.

They lost him on the table for two and a half minutes, but Jeremy came back. While in ICU, he started screaming, then crashed again. At that point, they pushed a cocktail of pain meds on him and revived him after he'd coded the second time, which sent him into anaphylactic shock. He was allergic to the medicines they'd administered. Yet my husband was doing what the Lord had directed me to tell him to do: Fight!

Later, Jeremy told me of his near-death experience. It was absolutely astonishing that he could tell me exactly where I was—in the waiting room where I was holding our youngest daughter, who was only seven months old at the time, and what was going on around him. He could see the medical professionals working on his body.

Most interesting, throughout his out-of-body experience, Jeremy met his son, who was miscarried from a previous relationship. He said he told his son, "It's not time yet. I have to go back."

Because of my own near-death experience—the car accident that took Momma from me—I believed every vivid detail Jeremy described. I get goose bumps thinking about the reunion we will all have when we are called home. What more could Christians ask for than to be with God and among those who've gone before us, but whose spirit remains like magnets forever clinging to our heart—even those we never had the opportunity to meet on Earth because they died at or before birth.

As lovely as the thoughts of Heaven, I had to shift my mind back to our real-life dilemma. Because of his injuries and surgeries, Jeremy became non-deployable and was on convalescent care for three or four months. What he feared most had become a reality.

Not only did we have Jeremy's medical issues to deal with, I was forced to resign from my job. My employer gave an option. "We have to have someone here. So either you resign or we will have to let you go."

I didn't want to be fired so I chose to quit. Our daughter was eight months old, and I was still nursing her. My priority was to be at home with my child and to take care of my husband.

During this time Obama was in office. Whether or not you like him, it doesn't matter. But I' m going to tell you what his policies did to my husband and other men and women who served in the military at that time.

Obama and the "powers that be" in what I call "the criminal initiative," would force my active duty Airman out of the military due to his injuries that he sustained in combat zones instead of allowing him to continue in his service to his country in an already non-deployable position in direct support of the Squadron Commander. The initiative punished our men and women who had served in the wars and conflicts.

They were going to deny and strip Jeremy of his rank that he was being promoted to. His "sew-on" date or "line badge number" was fast approaching at that time. At almost sixteen years of service, they were going to separate him without benefits. Criminal to say the least. What a great thank you to a man who served his country with utmost honor and bravery?

So I said, "No. I'm not going to put up with this." I went to two of his commanders, who basically stepped out of alignment to fight. The end result: my husband did sew on his rank the day of his retirement. And what ended up happening was he witnessed—he didn't actually do this himself— but he witnessed other troops and other friends of his that were getting their ranks literally ripped off from them for similar reasons.

With that, I saw such a great need to fight for our military and their families. Our children are nineteen and fifteen now, and they have been with us through all the surgeries. They helped me provide caregiving services when their dad was still in his hospital bed.

It's enough for the caregiving spouse to endure, but I saw the horror and the trauma that children of veterans suffer as well along with all of these disconnects within military active duty.

As we transitioned into civilian life, what did that look like? My husband and I fell through every single crack at the VA and during his time in service. We were determined that we were not going to let this happen to anyone else.

My neatly polished and pristine fingernails turned into a set of sharp claws. After everything I'd been through my entire life, every personal battle I'd fought, every health struggle I'd seen my husband suffer through, every personal loss and/or defeat I'd duked out with man and with Satan, I wasn't going to tolerate our veterans getting screwed by our own government.

Punishing our soldiers for having been wounded was adding insult to injury, and I vowed the government wasn't going to get away with it.

Dressed in civilian clothing, I was prepared to march onto the battlefield and wage war against the unfair policies the United States Government was stripping from our veterans.

The memory from the car accident came back into play. God told me on September 19th, 1994 that I had a choice. I could accompany Mom into Heaven, or I could return to Earth. If I chose to go back, I had a governmental call upon my life. But first, I had unfinished business elsewhere.

CHAPTER TWENTY-THREE

THERE WAS ONGOING drama between me and my biological father. Sometimes I got the feeling I mirrored Mom so much that Dad punished me for whatever unfinished business he had with her. Maybe he was still bitter with Mom for fleeing with me for her safety and mine, and residing hundreds of miles away. I can't prove that to be true, though.

As unfortunate as it was, when I got divorced from my first husband, my own dad took my ex's side in court and tried to keep my first-born daughter away from me. Talk about a gut punch. That wound ran deep. Once again, I was in the fight of my life—with my own blood-kin.

My biological father wasn't always honest, and I watched him consume a lot of alcohol. He would yell at me and verbally abuse me. I mean, maybe somewhere inside of him, he did love me—and I would hold that thought dear to my heart— but the constant put-downs didn't make me feel adored like a daughter should. Just seems Dad should have known how damaging it would be to my child—and to me—to lose custody. Then again, was that the big rub? Did he want me to feel the pain he felt when Mom took me and left him? I have no answer.

During the court proceedings, the judge caught Dad fibbing. It was so embarrassing that both of my grandfathers' got up and walked out of the courtroom, but neither of them uttered a word to me. I wanted so badly to tell them the truth one day regarding my ex-husband, but they both passed away before I ever could. My comfort is they know the untold story now—both are in Heaven.

I would take crap from Dad, and then I'd get enough and walk away. Like sticking your hand back in the fire after you'd already been burned, I kept going back and asking for more. He would hurt me again, and then I'd stop talking to him.

It was always stupid stuff like when my stepmom's father died, my youngest daughter was two years old. I was going to drive up to the funeral. But Dad told everyone that my daughter was unruly and horrible. He basically made it up because— at the age of two—my daughter was still too young to be labeled a holy terror. Besides that, Dad wasn't even around my youngest daughter enough times to know how well she behaved.

Thankfully, another family member finally saw the light. It was music to my ears when he one day said to me, "Lynz, I can't believe I didn't see all of this. They are lying about you." I can't express how relieved I was that someone else saw through it.

After some time would pass, Dad would get in touch with me and say, "Lynz, you need to stop throwing your family away."

That's the opposite of how I felt. I would argue that my dad was the one to throw me away.

Every single time, I would cave and return because I wanted the family unit to work. I wanted to experience and believe that—although no family is perfect—I could find some balance and normalcy and maintain a relationship. I didn't want to be shattered and scattered glass.

But then Dad would do dumb things again like telling my grandparents—both of his sets of grandparents—that I had married a drug dealer. Jeremy, an Air Force Airman and combat veteran was no drug dealer. He was more like an Apostle of Christ.

The lie he told about Jeremy backfired because when we came down from North Dakota— where we were stationed—and met my paternal grandparents, they saw that Jeremy was in the Air Force and was an upstanding man. Like me, they couldn't help but fall in love with him.

Dad tried spewing another tale, and that was the death knell when he said, "Well, you know Lynz's history. Kerry raised her." Kerry was my mom. "So she probably lied about what happened to her in Tennessee."

For my own dad to think that I would make up a story about a three hundred pound uncle, fifteen years my senior, throwing himself on top of me nearly every day for three years—and raping me—was his biggest insult ever.

That's when I realized that what he could never pin on Mom when he got angry, he would try and pin on me. Through his eyes, I was a carbon copy of her. And I will live my entire life believing Dad saw so many shades of Mom in me, that it would make him love me and then—at certain times—hate me.

All throughout my second marriage, I'd kept trying to transform a dysfunctional relationship with my dad into a functional one.

By this time, Jeremy was fed up with it himself. I spent so much time stewing over things Dad said and did, always wondering if I could recover from his 'last' comment.

Sitting in the kitchen, Jeremy asked me, "Lynz, Are you done yet?"

I guess he'd heard me rant and rave enough.

I stopped in my tracks. His comment resonated in a way that even the psychologist's questions hadn't. What was I getting in return besides stress, aggravation, and frustration? So why was I continuing to put up with the drama? Nothing had changed, and it certainly didn't appear it was going to.

Every time I returned and tried to make it work, it was like walking down the family sidewalk and always falling into the same old cracks. The frustrations and aggravations were not worth the stress, and the last thing I wanted was for it to cause trouble with my marriage.

I was still in deep thought when Jeremy said, "You don't have to do this. You don't have to live like this. It's not your fault. You did everything you could. Are you done yet?"

Once again, he assured me, "You don't have to live in this chaos anymore."

It was literally as if God was speaking through Jeremy.

I made the hard decision to separate from my paternal family—from my biological father.

Psychologists and psychiatrists would label it "emotional shielding," which is when a person throws up a barrier and distances themselves to prevent further pain and suffering.

Not to knock psychologists because they work wonders for so many people, but it didn't work for me. The professionals I sought help from wanted to hold me prisoner to my pain, and I was so ready to kick it to the curb and start anew. Spiritual healing is what worked for me. Through the help and the power of the Holy Spirit, I adopted Deuteronomy 7:26: "And you shall not bring an abominable thing into your house and become devoted to destruction like it. You shall utterly detest and abhor it, for it is devoted to destruction."

I had to protect my family, raise them up in the Lord as my momma raised me. Just as God watches over his children, I have to keep careful watch over my husband and daughters.

CHAPTER TWENTY-FOUR

THE DOCTORS KEPT telling us that eventually Jeremy would be in a wheelchair permanently. Much to our dismay, that day arrived; however, my husband swore it would be temporary.

Back before it was popular to share a tell-all story on Facebook—and with my husband's blessing—I wrote and posted Jeremy's entire ordeal in an open letter to Obama on the social media site.

Sometimes you have to cast pride aside and lay the truth on the line even if it feels like one million needles being driven through a medium-sized pincushion.

My husband was not embarrassed that I shared all of his issues with Post Traumatic Stress Disorder, his injuries, not to mention the fact that these disorders he'd suffered resulted in us having to sleep in separate beds.

Out of our very real and raw vulnerability, the letter went viral. Scores of people were not only touched by Jeremy's story, but having endured the same hardships, they related to it as well.

We were connected with people outside of the VA who were able to help us. For instance, the VA wouldn't pay for Jeremy to have a wheelchair; he had to have a special-fit wheelchair. The VA wouldn't pay for paddles so he could drive with his hands when he couldn't use his legs. What a disgrace when they even refused to provide service dogs. And these are services our government—was and is— supposed to provide. I was livid with the benefits Jeremy and other veterans were being denied. I'm not too proud to admit, I was like a tiger in the wild. I made phone calls, demanded meetings and answers as to why they were stripping the military from benefits earned and well-deserved.

It's always important—and I would encourage anyone suffering the same or similar difficulties— to keep a meticulously written record because documentation of every single phone call, meeting, and correspondence demanding fairness throughout the process is vital to proving your efforts to seek justice.

When it comes to seeing things through to fruition, it's very easy to understand the old phrase, "It takes an act of Congress." To get anything passed, to make any headway whatsoever, to get attention and cooperation from the government is a long and drawn-out process. I roll my eyes because it's a battle veterans shouldn't have to combat. They are America's prized possession and should be treated as such.

It was so amazing and well worth our fight to see enormous amounts of people get an instant breakthrough, which took Jeremy and I jumping through many hoops and hurdles in order to spare others from facing the same hardships.

I didn't have an organization. I wasn't getting paid. We just started because people would contact me and Jeremy. We met with different leaders (elected, appointed, and non-profit) from across the nation and people would call us and ask, "How did you do that?"

And I would say, "Well, this didn't work. That did work. This is who you need to talk to, because as a caregiver, we kept records of everything."

From there, it began to branch out.

CHAPTER TWENTY-FIVE

WHEN I WAS thirteen, I'd traveled to Charleston, South Carolina, and I fell in love with its charm. There was a pull and an energy that seemed to always direct and draw me back. I also recall on that visit, God telling me I would one day live in Charleston.

Lo and behold, when Jeremy lost his job in Utah, we moved to the Lowcountry, which just happened to be the only city in the entire country where Jeremy was offered a job. Not only that, the first house we purchased was a house that was a reproduction of the homes on Rainbow Row, and the price was slashed twenty thousand dollars. Rainbow—a promise from God! How incredible.

I was working in downtown Charleston in an office. It was a common space. And this gentleman, who'd heard and read about Jeremy via the multiple Facebook shares, said to me, "Hey! Your story with the caregiver program, there is actually an organization with Senator Elizabeth Dole. I know the current South Carolina Dole Fellow, and you should apply for this."

Senator Elizabeth Dole hand selects Fellows every two years to represent each state. Some states have more than one. Fellows are leaders in their communities who share their caregiving stories to bring vital attention to the tremendous challenges caregivers face, and they provide care to a wounded warrior.

My husband will say, "A veteran with a disability," but he's not disabled because he doesn't see himself as handicapped or a throwaway. Jeremy is a priceless gem.

We never know who God will use, or how God will use us. My encounter with a stranger prompted me to apply for the Elizabeth Dole Fellow. I was more than honored when I was accepted.

Through the Dole Caregiver Fellowship, we—as caregivers—receive support, training, and a platform to address the issues impacting the community. We share our stories directly with national leaders and decision makers within the business, entertainment, faith, and nonprofit sectors to transform the culture of care in our country.

In 2018, I was put into contact with an international statesman. I spent a year training and shadowing with him. As an international stateswoman, I traveled to different embassies, one of them being a South Sudanese Embassy in

Kampala. And I was brought in through veterans, civility, and humanitarian work via different embassies and worked with different leaders.

It was a real eye-opener to discover in some of these nations, Kings of Tribes, at times, would settle disputes by chopping others heads off. In my work as a stateswoman, we go in with civility and say, "Hey! Treat us the way that you want to be treated without compromising value of who the person is across from you—or in our case in America, our Constitution."

We can still have civility by firmly stating, "I'm not going to compromise our Constitution and our Christian values, but I can still treat you the way that you want to be treated. It's a mutual exchange."

The knowledge and experience I gained as a stateswoman is part of my story. But that isn't nearly the end of it.

CHAPTER TWENTY-SIX

A S A STATESWOMAN visiting with leaders of our country as well as others around the world, I've seen and observed a lot. I've sat at the table with people holding office in America, whom I personally feel are not authentic or real. Some are draped in humility. But more of them have an elitist, superiority air about them.

People in government positions are not better than the ordinary citizen. They are not below us either. We are all created equal. And that one statement alone binds me to the United States Constitution, which I hold dear to my heart. I vow to uphold the principles of life, liberty and the pursuit of happiness that our founding fathers set in place for America. These are the birthrights given her.

The problems we are facing in our country are not confined to the Republican party nor can the Democrats be solely blamed. Corruption runs deep on both sides of the aisle, which has placed us in an American crisis. The majority of the time, there is so much mudslinging taking place on the taxpayers' dime, it's nothing but a pork waste.

I can't erase from my mind what I've learned as a stateswoman. Financial waste, open borders, human trafficking, money laundering and election theft are among a few.

Because of the evidence that's been uncovered, the scores of people who turned out to vote in the 2020 election, the thousands of people who showed up for President Trump's rallies—not just before the 2020 election but to this day—it is more than obvious to me that our 2020 election was stolen from our 45th president. More importantly, the election was stolen from We the People.

And I don't care if publicly stating that ticks anybody off. It is the truth. The media and a majority of our government will try to gaslight citizens and have them believe otherwise, but there is another set of fact-checkers who can solidly prove them wrong. The ones who hold the truth are not given credence, which is unfair and a major injustice to We the People.

Another bone I have to pick is the United States is a Republic, not a Democracy. Yet it's no secret—and if it is, it shouldn't be and it's time to wake up—that we have many elected officials vying to change and/or eliminate our Constitution, which could very well strip us of our rights if we don't take a stand and fight against it. If communism works its way in, America is gone forever. We cannot allow this to happen.

I believe a leader is first and always a servant serving people. For example, when I go to church or visit my pastors, they are always serving other people. The incredible leaders I've met with get up, get off their behind, and they serve people first before they are served. That's important for everyone to remember.

It's fascinating that a friend of mine designed my logo, which actually looks like a crown. It has five stars. And these five stars represent the five pillars of God's character. If that doesn't indicate it's time the people rest on the shoulders of humility, I don't know what does.

Through humility, this is the greatest form of God's nature because the Lord laid Himself down because He wanted to be in relationship with us. And so out of that comes the second pillar, which is a pure form of integrity. The third is a sacred culture of honor. The fourth is civility—treating others the way you want to be treated. And the fifth is service. In an excerpt of John 14:12, Jesus says, "Greater things than Me will you do." I believe that is the greatest leadership statement of all time.

All of these concerns led me into deep thought about the future of America and what I could do to make our country a better place for our children and our children's-children and generations to come.

CHAPTER TWENTY-SEVEN

AFTER THE WORD had circulated regarding my fight for the rights of veterans, I had friends locally and across the nation saying, "Hey! You need to run for office." I had seriously considered it, but I needed more of a nudge. I needed for God to speak it to me clearly.

The first nudge was my previous opponent's response to the 2020 election wherein she did not acknowledge that the 2020 election had been stolen from the American people. If that wasn't enough, she blamed President Trump for the events of January 6th, without—to this day—providing proof, which is unfair, unjust, unconstitutional, and un-American. We still have political prisoners who have not had the right to a trial by jury.

The second and final confirmation of my decision came when I received a message from a former high ranking government official—General Michael Flynn—asking me to run for office. It was then I decided to run for Congress in South Carolina's District One.

In doing so, I received death threats, had lies spread about me, which caused more drama than a multitude of screenwriters could ever concoct for a TV series. But that didn't stop me nor will it prevent me from continuing to pursue my governmental endeavors. Choosing to represent my district and country far outweighs the threats upon my life and the unnecessary theater that goes along with a grassroots public campaign.

The major issues that I ran on were election integrity, border crises, trafficking, and parental rights and education. If we don't find out how the election was stolen and who did it, if people think the price of inflation, gas, tyranny and other problems we have now are massive, I regret to state: you haven't seen anything yet.

We're already suffering to the point of ruination under the Biden administration. We can't afford to wait for the midterm elections. Our fight is now, and time is of the essence.

I'm afraid the people who are content with the outcome of the 2020 election will one day regret they didn't fight for a free and fair election, especially if it causes Americans to lose our sovereignty. That's my spirit of discernment kicking into overdrive from what I've seen as a stateswoman, fellow, and with my experience on the campaign trail.

The good news is that people are not only waking up in the state of South Carolina, but also across America with multiple leaders who are listening. The anomalies found are mind-boggling. As a result of audits being done across the country, a good majority of the American people are demanding restitution and justice for what happened in 2020 and ongoing.

A colleague of mine described his analogy. If you own a business and someone stole fifty thousand dollars from you—and let's say you have twenty employees—are you going to be able to trust those employees if you can't ever track where that money went? No. You're not going to be able to trust them, and you're going to need for someone to investigate and find out where the fifty thousand dollars went.

One way we can eliminate theft of our election is using the following: 1. paper ballots. (A great representation would be the watermarked paper ballot designed and suggested by Arizona representative Mark Finchem), 2. one day elections and also marked as a federal holiday; 3. paper poll books, and paper ballot reconciliation. (We need to clean the voter rolls).

Aside from the election solutions, we also need to audit the fed and institute a national flat sales tax to be handled by each state respectively.

There are too many foxes guarding the henhouse. It's time the taxpaying citizens demand accountability with how our finances are being handled—or mishandled.

The President doesn't have the power. Congress doesn't have the power. The power resides with We the People. And we must refuse to be governed in tyranny by leaders who are committing treason and misappropriating our funds. We need to find the root of all the sinister acts taking place within the confines of our government, expose it and then dispose of every level of corruption.

And while we're at it, I believe our second amendment rights to bear arms. No restrictions. I believe we should have a non-federalized reciprocity across the nation. No registry.

CHAPTER TWENTY-EIGHT

THE US BORDER crisis and trafficking is of major concern, and it should be to every American. In the past year and a half, I've been to the border twice. It takes a week-long visit to fully grasp the everyday occurrences happening on United States soil. It's horrific, despicable, inhumane and underreported—if reported at all. When President Trump was in office, he was testing the DNA of immigrants who were coming over the border. His method of operation determined these so-called families were not related, a strong indication they were being trafficked.

Unfortunately, there is no DNA testing being done under the Biden administration. Having open doors is causing major sores for Americans due to the illegal aliens pouring through in record numbers. The very people—namely, the Federal Government—who needs to solve this problem is actually causing the crisis. They could do something about it, but they don't.

A lot of government leaders hop on a plane and fly to the border long enough to have a thirty minute photo-op, and that's the extent of their time and effort. They are not really finding out what's going on. And if they do know, they don't tell or they flat out fib about it.

The horrific occurrences at our border pains me to the depths of my existence. Women are told they are going to be raped. If they fight being raped, they are told they will be murdered. Children are being drugged with Dramamine, then raped. Why do you think there is so many drugs laced with Fentanyl coming from our border? And that only explains one reason—money being the other.

If being drugged and raped isn't bad enough, the drug thugs then hang the undergarments of the women and children they've raped on the trees as a trophy. That should infuriate the entire world population. The green vegetation God gave us to shield and protect has been labeled "rape trees." Their actions are pathetic; getting away with their crimes is equally worse.

The women and children are also, at times, tattooed or branded. Or they have bracelets they wear to determine how they will be trafficked, what they will be used for, and where they are being trafficked to. I have shot some footage of the border. The gates are wide open. What the cartels are getting away with is criminally insane. Americans need to stop being afraid of the ones who actually work for us. The government wouldn't financially exist if it wasn't for We the People bankrolling their salaries. Remember that when they try to enforce "mandates"—dates determined by man to achieve their own agenda. The US Constitution protects our sovereignty, and we are under no duty by man to comply.

I've been against the mandates since 2020. From inside my office in downtown Charleston where my business was located at that time, I witnessed people—who weren't law enforcement officers—going from business to business without a search warrant issuing tickets to patrons, employees, and to business owners for not wearing masks, which is against the law and the United States Constitution.

Then they would bully these business owners by stating, "You have to see us in court—trial by jury." It was like a three-ring circus or a kangaroo court because these aren't licensed police officers. One of my favorite books is titled *Doctrine of the Lesser Magistrates* by Matthew J. Trewhella. The author takes you back through different times in history where the lesser magistrate, which would be like a sheriff or a state leader or even governors, would stand in the gap against the overreach, wherever that overreach is occurring. For example—what's happening right now— they should have been standing up for us in South Carolina and across America. But it has taken months of this communist regime and all of the erupting chaos for them to finally stand up and say, "Oh, we need to do something about this."

Had they been involved from the beginning and jumped in before this became out-of-control government overreach, we would have the solution, not the problem.

For safety purposes, most everyone keeps the doors of their homes and cars locked because they don't want strangers and criminals entering at leisure. The same rules need to apply for the United States Border.

In the midst of all the chaos, I have been in the trenches fighting. I show up at school board meetings, city council meetings, and working with people, not just in this district, but across the state and the nation. I have been turned away and locked out of certain meetings at various places because I refuse to comply with the mandates. I am exercising my constitutional rights. Everyone else should be doing the same because what God says about freedom is written in Peter 2:15-16: "Act as free men, and do not use your freedom as a covering for evil, but use it as bondslaves of God."

God doesn't want us to be slaves to men, and His Word supports defending our freedoms from evil and tyranny. In order to turn a corner in this country, we have to turn back to God—not turn our back on God. America was founded on Biblical principles, and the US Constitution will absolutely be upheld on my watch.

CHAPTER TWENTY-NINE

MY CAMPAIGN WAS always about grassroots, which isn't the usual campaign where millions of dollars are raised and the candidate is endorsed by big names. I liken my movement to the ministry of Jesus Christ. His entire ministry wasn't contained in the church. It actually spread outside the church, and it was powerful because His entire movement was grassroots.

Jesus freely traveled about speaking to the people. He didn't have to put out a name for himself or build a platform. He simply walked in humility and truth. People are drawn to truth because it doesn't lie. Truth doesn't mislead. The truth sets us free.

Now don't get me wrong. With a campaign, you do have to put your name out there and register. I understand that. But grassroots is a component of two things: connection and relationship. A successful grassroots movement is going to connect with people through ideas—and not always the same idea. We bring our differences to the table, and we build relationships through sharing. The combination of minds is where reasoning, logic and unity take place.

When I initially meet someone, there is that connection. I may not hop around and say, "Hi! I'm Lynz. I'm running for Congress. I'll see you later." And then I move on to the next one. I want to take that moment—even if it costs me people walking away—to speak with you or whoever is in front of me about their concerns.

I'll ask, "What do you need? How can I serve you? What is going on?"

I am not better than anybody else. But I will tell you I was the first candidate who stepped up, and I will continue to fight with and for We the People. And we will continue to stand in the gap and fight for our Constitution, our individual states and our nation.

At a Boeing event I attended, I asked questions of people. "Do you work here? Do you have family members working here? Do you need doctors? Do you need attorneys? What do you need? How can we help you?"

Government leaders are supposed to serve the people. Somehow through the years, they hoodwinked us into believing the opposite. Through a complete and total mind game, we got played.

It is crucial that we regain control of our country now—before it's too late. And this won't happen unless the people get involved.

General Flynn has a motto that I love and use: "Local involvement equals national impact."

There are many different grassroots movements where people can get involved in different states. There are election integrity groups, medical groups, legal, educational and anti-trafficking coalitions. If you can't find a group, start one. Grassroots can spread like wildfire.

CHAPTER THIRTY

WHETHER YOU'RE A parent or not, this is important: Everyone should be concerned with what I refer to as the "transdemic."

For starters, if you don't believe or you are unaware that this is playing out in our public school systems, you can visit *www.themindpolluters.com* and watch the documentary produced by Fearless Features. What these whistleblowers reveal—and God bless them for stepping forward—will literally blow your mind.

Most parents are hard at work and trust the education system to teach in the same manner they were taught, but I can't emphasize enough: pay very close attention to how the groundwork has been laid via online curriculum and textbooks. Pedophilia is not normal, nor will it ever become an accepted standard as long as We the People fight against this evil and felonious lifestyle the Left is trying to normalize. Sadly, children are easy prey, and they can quickly become a victim if we sit back and wait for a broken system to repair itself. Have you ever known broken to fix itself? No. Repairs are always necessary, and the time is now to take a stand and become a repairman or a repairwoman.

Every parent needs to research "Social Emotional Learning." It is true that our children are being indoctrinated beginning as young as four years of age—using a sly and sneaky way of pushing their Trans Agenda. Kids need to learn reading, writing, arithmetic and American history, not about their genitalia and masturbation. Or, worse, sexualizing child pornography; it's downright criminal.

Do you want teachers confusing your children about the sex God gave to them? I would hope you answer no to that question. Since the beginning of time, women have given birth to either a boy or a girl. In some cases, it might be twin girls, twin boys or a twin boy and girl—or triplets.

You might wonder why on Earth I would even make such a statement. It is to inform everyone about another disaster happening in our public school systems—the "Furry Phenomenon."

Across the United States, students are dressing as dogs, cats, wolves, and other animals. The cat students are meowing at other students and scaring them out of their wits. Students dressed as dogs are barking. The student wolves are howling. This is such abnormal behavior and is far beyond what God intended. All of this indoctrination is a means of grooming for traffickers who prey on the vulnerabilities of our children.

Women have never given birth to dogs, cats, wolves or anything other than human beings. Can you name one man who has *ever* given birth to a child? No—because men don't have birth canals. The furry phenomenon can be found by visiting *https://pubmed.ncbi.nlm.nih.gov/30806867/*.

Furthermore, men do not belong in the bathroom with women. That can open the door for sexual harassment and rape. It should also be of grave concern with students trying to morph into animals.

How would you feel if you encountered someone in the women's bathroom who is dressed as an animal? I would be more than a wee bit freaked out, and I shiver at the thought of a child encountering a furry while in a public restroom—so should any parent. Furthermore, we shouldn't even have to be concerned with this behavior. It's creepy, beyond ridiculous and was impossible to imagine this becoming a reality as recent as a decade ago.

The bottom line: Man is trying to complicate what God made simple. Genesis 1:27 says, "So God created man in his own image, in the image of God he created him; male and female he created them." Period. End of story.

I can preach a sermon for hours on end, but I can't solve the problem solo. We the People are the solution, and We the People need to get involved now—not later—if we want to save America from the demonic and satanic influences that are working overtime to groom our children into being something that is not of their own choosing. This unnatural behavior is being peddled and marketed in disguise by dark influencers.

We are in spiritual warfare whether you want to believe it or not. This is a battle of good versus evil, and these demonic forces are manufacturing one crisis after another to keep us in a state of lockdown so they can maintain control. It has to stop, but ending it starts with us. Otherwise, we are ushering in communism at record pace.

Gaslighting the public and instilling fear into the people has to stop as well. And it begins with not complying. As far as mandates, masks do not work. Vaccines are emergency use authorization only and are not proven to work. In fact, the efficacy and safety of vaccines is in question.

It's a real shocker when many healthcare professionals have never even heard of *www.openvaers.com*. That is a government website, which provides the numbers of deaths and injuries reported by the vaccinated. Last check, there have been over two million deaths and injuries reported on patients who were vaccinated—and only one percent are listed.

I'm further fueled and motivated to keep this grassroots movement in forward motion when we receive messages from as far away as Japan. Their leaders—their people—are so excited. They said to me, "Your campaign is reaching us over here, and it is encouraging us. Please keep fighting. Don't give up."

Being silenced as a child has resulted in me screaming the truth out loud as an adult. People need to know what is unfolding before our very eyes. We've got to reverse course in America or we will no longer have a country, which led me to write *I Am Silent No More*.

CHAPTER THIRTY-ONE

I GET ASKED ALL the time by people who know or hear about my past, "How can you be so strong and resilient after what you endured?"

It's not *what* healed me; it is *He* who healed me— God. I didn't want to be a victim anymore, but at the time, I was clearly aware that I was. I'm not just a survivor, I am an overcomer.

Overcoming is just a matter of walking out the journey. Anyone can be healed by and through the grace of God, but we first have to come into alignment with Him.

The amount of money I do or don't have in the bank, being raped or not being raped, being trafficked or not being trafficked does not define me. None of that changes my identity in Christ because I'm still seated in Heavenly places. These bad things did happen to me, but they don't have to be my story. I set my story.

God defines me and He has a plan for my life and for your life.

I reference Psalm 139:13-18.

> ¹³ For you created my inmost being;
>   you knit me together in my mother's womb.
> ¹⁴ I praise you because I am fearfully and
>   wonderfully made;
>   your works are wonderful,
>   I know that full well.
> ¹⁵ My frame was not hidden from you
>   when I was made in the secret place,
>   when I was woven together in the depths of
>   the earth.
> ¹⁶ Your eyes saw my unformed body;
>   all the days ordained for me were written
>   in your book before one of them came to
>   be.
> ¹⁷ How precious to me are your
>   thoughts,[a] God!
>   How vast is the sum of them!
> ¹⁸ Were I to count them,
>   they would outnumber the grains of sand—
>   when I awake, I am still with you.

I didn't want to walk as a victim the rest of my life. I didn't want to live in despair. Doing so was interacting with and leaving me in the darkness. For many, staying in dark corners can become a habitual place of comfort and a way of life. But then we realize we don't like being there and it doesn't feel right, so we break free by stepping into the Light of Christ.

I used to ask, "God, why did all these things happen to me when I was a kid?"

And He said, "You're asking the wrong question. What can you do from this? What can you learn from this?"

Time will pass by, and your destiny will be locked up by your own choice that you hold the key to. It's like trying to drive a car blindfolded. You're going to end up in a worse situation—or inflict your pain onto someone else—until you step out in faith with a will and a determination to overcome victimization so you can move forward. With God there are no accidents. Mistakes are not in his wheelhouse. Silence is not an option. Standing up for God is mandatory. Esther 4:14: "If you persist in staying silent at a time like this, help and deliverance will arrive for the Jews from someplace else; but you and your family will be wiped out. Who knows? Maybe you were made queen for just such a time as this."

CHAPTER THIRTY-TWO

BACK TO MY family and all the dysfunctions from my childhood, I conclude.

I never talk to Aunt Ursula or my uncle. Several years after I'd left their home and my uncle entered a plea bargain, I learned transporting an individual—in my case a minor—across state lines for the exchange of money and forcing them to have sex is called human trafficking.

The sexual assaults began before I was adopted. I considered myself a victim of human trafficking, and I became a strong and determined advocate for victims' rights.

In 2020, I felt a spiritual tug. As valuable as it was and had been to me throughout my life, I gave up Momma's Bible. With a handwritten note that read, "You need this more than I do," I mailed it to Aunt Ursula. I never heard back. I didn't expect to. That chapter of my life is finished, and I have forgiven it.

Where am I with my biological father? That was then and this is now. Instead of disliking my dad's behavior and berating him for unfair treatment toward me, I have forgiven him as well. After all,

I am his other half and he is the man God chose to be my father.

So aside from the many injustices, misunderstandings—and for those times we didn't see eye to eye—I owe him a debt of gratitude for rescuing me from the uncle who turned my world upside down and inside out by raping and enslaving me.

I forgive my biological father for the mistakes he's made because he is imperfect.

I've seen how the justice system works. People lie. And my uncle could have easily made it appear as if I had consented to having sexual relations with him. He tried to make me believe it. Had that happened, it would have added insult to injury in ways I don't even want to imagine.

With a plea bargain, my uncle admitted what he did was wrong. And if that's the most that came from it, then it was much better than an acquittal. It must have been like rolling dice. No one can predict what side the cube will land.

And that must have also been how my paternal grandparents felt when they took me in at the age of sixteen. They were trying to help and understand a sixteen year old granddaughter they didn't really know or raise overcome a tragedy that they had nothing to do with.

As a daughter of Christ, I can't help but love my dad even though we've had our share of differences. The same grace and love that Jesus has for me, I extend to him.

My wounded combat Veteran husband, once confined to a wheelchair, now walks again! In 2018, we visited Little River Baptist Church in North Carolina. Jeremy heard the audible voice of God say, "If you get up and walk, your legs will work."

I kid you not: he rolled himself down to the altar. He stood up, and when he did, he could feel the heat from the tips of his toes all the way up to his hips. He proved the doctors wrong. For over four years now, Jeremy has been walking on his own two legs. He never gave up, and that's inspired me to never give up. His resilience is amazing. God heals. Believe it!

As unfortunate as it was that I lost my mom at a young age and was in the car with her when she died, I believe—with every fiber of my being— that Mom mounted up on God's shoulders when she drew her last breath on Earth and became an integral part of me living out my destiny interceding for me in the cloud of witnesses. I truly believe she has helped the Lord carry me through life. Though the spelling is different, it's ironic that Mom's name is Kerry. *Kerry* me!

I never touched the keys on the piano after I played the Sandy Patty song at Mom's memorial service. That was the day the music died. Now I just might sit down at the piano again and hit a few notes. Think I'll start with "How Great Thou Art!"

THE END!

BECOME AN OVERCOMER
STUDY GUIDE AND EXERCISES
BY LYNZ PIPER-LOOMIS:

THROUGHOUT THE LAST nearly forty years of my life, I have witnessed and endured many tragedies, AND I have also seen and experienced even yet, greater joy. The evil one meant to take my life out. However, the Lord decided—as He does for each of us—that He has a plan for our lives.

I came to terms with my past, and I vow to not ever allow my past to define my present or my future. Someone once told me I would never finish anything, and that I could not do what I had set my mind to. I defied their words and ran straight ahead for the race marked out for me (Hebrews 12:1). God does not ask us to know it all. He just asks us for our full surrender, obedience, and to leave fear behind. (Jeremiah 1) The Lord led me through Seven Steps of Healing, Forgiveness, and Overcoming. I pray that they will impart into you the same fire that I have had all of these years and that you will take action. The world needs you and your solutions. I will leave you with this final quote before we embark into your new adventure waiting below. Let your tragedy, your joy, your tears, as well as your failures fuel the fire within you to overcome.

"Success is the ability to go from one failure to another with no loss of enthusiasm."
    ~Sir Winston Churchill

STEP ONE: AWARENESS

AWARENESS IS KEY. I was aware before that I was a victim. I thought I felt comfortable sitting in that position until I shifted my awareness away from being a victim, and I saw that there was Someone's hand reaching down to grab mine.

As I climbed out of the place I thought I was comfortable, I became more keenly aware that the place I was in represented death. There was no life there. The longer I climbed the mountain of overcoming, I realized that my place of pain was not a place for me to gain life. Instead, it was in a place of discomfort that I overcame and flourished.

We must have keen "awareness" of our position. We must evaluate our heart posture internally. Brokenness yields more brokenness. Wholeness yields more wholeness.

John 16:33 ESV, "I have said these things to you, that in me you may have peace. In the world you will have tribulation. But take heart; I have overcome the world.

1) What is my heart posture? Am I a victim? Am I an overcomer? Evaluate your mindset. Write below what your current heart posture is. Are you ready to do "an about face", and leave behind the place in the valley?

Reach up, there is a hand waiting to hoist you up your mountain of overcoming.

2) Next, time to pray.

Lord, I fully surrender my heart to You. I was aware that was a victim. I see now that You do not define me as a victim. You never had it in Your plan for me to walk in brokenness. Lord, I thank You that You created me in Your image, and that You have promised to never leave me nor forsake me. I want to begin today to believe in who You say I am. I am an overcomer. Thank You, Lord. Amen.

3) Take a moment to sit still and write down what you are experiencing.

STEP TWO: AUTHENTICITY

WHAT IS YOUR identity? Your Origin? How do I currently identify myself? Who am I really?

For years I defined myself, yes, as a victim. However, I also identified as anything separate from being a child of God. I mean, I said it. However, it was not the same as believing it. I was ready to lie down and die. I had no desire to live. As I mentioned in the pages of this book, I tried to take my life more than once.

So what is our origin? God created us in His image. (Genesis 1:26–27) He desired to have us as His children, and to be in relationship with us. I gave my life to Jesus at the age of four. However, I drifted, then returned and surrendered everything back to Him. It was in that moment I knew I was His. My origin came from Him, making and molding me with His hands and breathing His breath into my nostrils giving me life.

2 Corinthians 5:21 TPT: "For God made the only one who did not know sin to become sin for us, so that we might become the righteousness of God through our union with Him."

This is the very first step. John 3:16 says that, "For God so loved the world, that He gave His only begotten Son, that whosoever believeth in Him should not perish, but have everlasting life."

The first step to your journey is surrendering your life to Christ.

Have you ever given your life to Jesus? If not, now is the time. If so but you've drifted, it is time to surrender your life to Him once more.

If you have accepted Jesus already as your savior, then meditate on the scriptures above until the next session. The truth is that God sees you in His image, and not the brokenness of the evil one. If you have never given your life to Jesus or you want to surrender your life once more, pray this prayer with me.

Father, thank you for giving your Son on the cross as the ultimate sacrifice for my sins. I believe in Jesus Christ and ask today that He would come to dwell within my heart. I am sorry for my sin, and I thank You that You said in Your word that You have made me new. Thank you that I am now Your child. I choose this day whom to serve. I choose You. Amen.

Congratulations! Welcome to the body of Christ. You are made new—Authenticity!

After today's session, I would love for you to take a still moment to reflect on your experience via journaling or drawing. Begin reading Ephesians and watch God's words come to life in your life today!

STEP 3: ACKNOWLEDGMENT

ACKNOWLEDGMENT. NOW, THAT we are aware of our heart posture and our mindset. We acknowledge the past, AND now we must leave the past in the past. We must acknowledge that we want change. I acknowledged that I was victimized, BUT I wanted to avoid living in a constant state of denial. I said to myself, "I am going to acknowledge that I do not want to be a victim anymore."

I did not want to suffer from anorexia or bulimia anymore so I spoke it out of my existence and surrendered it to God. I asked Him to help me stop. I was desperate. I was immediately healed. Those issues I was suffering from ended right then and there.

Proverbs 3:5-6 ESV, "Trust in the Lord with all your heart, and do not lean on your own understanding. In all your ways acknowledge Him, and He will make straight your paths."

Prayer:
Lord, I no longer want to suffer from _____. I want to leave the past with the past. Thank You, Lord, that I can trust

in You with all my heart. Thank You for making straight my paths.

Question: Are you ready to leave the past behind you? It will more than likely require you to forgive someone, and maybe even yourself. I know this is THE hardest thing to do. It is quite frankly, the most difficult step.

However, you cannot move forward in your journey unless you are willing to forgive. The evil one does not want you to forgive because he loses. You gain peace, and the ability to push forward in your dreams and destiny that God has set forth for you.

It is also important to pray for that person and ask God to bless them. He desires that not one would perish and be separated from His love.

Write down the people that you know you need to forgive. When you are ready, pray this prayer below.

Lord, if I am being honest, this is hard. I need your help. I cannot do this without you. Father, I forgive
_____ for _____.
I am ready to leave the past in the past, and I am asking that you will move in the lives of those that have hurt me. I pray that they will have an opportunity for salvation through Your Son Jesus, and that they would never be separated from

Your love. Father, see to it that they are blessed as You desire. In Jesus' name, Amen.

Matthew 6:15, TPT: But if you withhold forgiveness from others, your Father withholds forgiveness from you."

Take a moment to reflect on what just happened. Sit and be still. Journal or draw afterwards what you experienced through this last session.

STEP 4: ALIGNMENT

THIS NEXT SESSION is going to evaluate the influences in and around you. We bear fruit in what we partake in. We bear fruit in what we speak. We bear fruit of those we allow to speak into our lives.

Proverbs 18:21, ESV: "Death and life are in the power of the tongue, and those who love it will eat its fruit."

This was a particularly difficult season for me. I dragged this season out for way too long. I wish I would have dug my heels in lieu of procrastinating. But I had to evaluate what and whom I was listening to who were influencing my life.

Have you heard the phrase, "You become the people you hang out with?" I evaluated those in my life that were speaking death into my life, and I evaluated my own tongue and the circumstances I was in at the time.

When I finally became obedient to God and purged myself of those influences, my circumstances changed. Let me be clear. Delayed obedience is still disobedience. I thought it would only affect me. However, my choices greatly impacted my relationship with my husband and my children. It affected my journey in life as well. I am not telling you to throw away your marriage or to throw friendships away. What I am saying is this: We need to be in the word of God in order to stay in alignment with the Lord. We need fresh revelation from Him in order that our world internally—within our hearts—stays on the path of overcoming.

What we put in our hearts via sight and hearing greatly affects how we align our world internally. I did have to severe a few relationships that were just downright gruesome. I also had to evaluate how I was speaking. Was I speaking life or death? We can tell by the fruit we bear.

My entire life shifted again when I came into alignment. It is time to ask God for his wisdom, understanding, counsel, and discernment. Are you ready?

Do you know the posture of your alignment? Are you speaking death or life? What type of fruit do you bear?

What are outside influences via what you watch and listen to? What type of fruit do they bear in general and in your life? What about relationships and counsel?

Prayer: Father, I am ready to come into alignment and to speak life and bear life fruit. I ask You for Your wisdom and discernment in order that I align my heart internally with Your heart. Thank You Father. Amen.

James 1:5, ESV: "If any of you lacks wisdom, let him ask God, who gives generously to all without reproach, and it will be given to him."

Take a moment to reflect on this session. How is God asking you to change your alignment to reflect His heart for you?

STEP FIVE: AUTHORITY

AS AN OVERCOMER, you have authority in what you have overcome. You can reach your hand down and help to hoist up another because your victory bears witness to breakthrough victory for another person. You are now qualified to take action because of what you have been through and because in Christ, we have the authority.

Luke 10:19, ESV: "Behold, I have given you authority to tread on serpents and scorpions, and over all the power of the enemy, and nothing shall hurt you."

Evaluate who is in your circle of influence or community around you that maybe walking through the same sufferings you endured. Your community is defined as those you do life with or connect with and have a relationship with. It goes back to the grassroots level.

Remember? Everything Jesus did was grassroots and was built upon that connection and relationship. There is someone near you that needs a breakthrough and your helping hand to see them through to the ultimate victory.

Who is that person? Write it down. Ask God to help you to help them. Ask God what He wants you to pray specifically for them.

Journal/draw in reflection of what you believe God is sharing with you about them for them.

STEP SIX: ACTIVATION

TAKE TIME AFTER the last session to connect with whomever you wrote down, and ask them if they would like to grab a cup of coffee with you or a bite to eat. Meeting in person is going to take you out of your comfort zone. Trust me.

After your call and your meet-up post this session, reflect in your journal or draw what became of this experience.

Now, evaluate a few things.
1. What do I have in common with this person? Is there something I have overcome that is similar to them?

2. Societal Sphere of Influence as defined by Meriam Webster Dictionary, "A territorial area within which the political influence or the interests of one nation are held to be more or less paramount."

3. Is there a societal sphere of influence we commonly share, are passionate about, live and work together in?

4. What am I passionate about? For me personally, I am passionate about government. I am passionate about the government being pure, righteous, and having correct not corrupt justice. I am passionate about the people being the governors instead of a government governing the people.

5. Activation happens daily. We activate ourselves into many different areas and issues. The issue remains: Are we called to activate in all of those areas?

I used to give people a piece of my mind—without a filter. Let me be honest. I filtered through my pain instead of a place of wholeness. It is okay to say no. In fact, you will find so much freedom in saying no. Your "yes" can then be directed and activated in what you were designed and created to be activated in.

Matthew 5:37, ESV: "Let what you say be simply 'yes' or 'no'; anything more than this comes from evil."

Prayer:
God, where shall I say no so that You can have my full yes? Where shall I say yes? Thank You for activating me in who You created me to be for such a time as this. Amen.

Write down the areas that God has said to say "no" to.

Write down again that one thing in your heart that keeps you up at night. That one thing you wish you could change. There is your "yes".

STEP SEVEN: ACTIONVISM

(Activism + Action = Actionvism)

NOW IT IS time to dream and put action to your activism. There are many people authoring books and just as many talking heads across the world. The line is drawn when we see the fruit of someone's activism. Activism without action is pointless.

Thus, the dictionary needs a new word! *Actionvism.* Activism plus action yields the fruit of ACTIONVISM. It is time for you to take your breakthrough plus passion to create your course of action.

Be still and write down some solutions for your breakthrough. How did you breakthrough in victory? I believe we are each individually a solution. Without each of us individually applying our solutions into this world, we are globally at a significant loss when one person passes without fulfilling their destiny.

Now, I want you to think about the people that may be of influence that you can partner with in order to move forward. Who are they?

I have both non-partisan and partisan issues I am working on. However, humanity suffers from these issues regardless of partisan views. I have to work with people whose views I sometimes despise in order to get the course of action completed. I never want my own agenda or opinions of people to get in the way of getting the course of action passed.

God will more than likely place us in a position where we are seated with those who oppose us. He gives us a seat at the table and an opportunity to influence and bring change when we lay ourselves down.

Psalm 23:5, ESV: "You prepare a table before me in the presence of my enemies."

Humility. Only through humility can we grow, mature, and promote to the next course of action. Humility is God's greatest form of His nature. It was through humility I forgave those who wronged me. It was through humility that I am where I am today. It is through humility that we sit at a table in the presence of our enemies. Never forget that the light always overcomes darkness. Pride always leads us to destruction.

John 1:5, ESV: "The light shines in the darkness, and the darkness has not overcome it."

Proverbs 6:18, ESV: "Pride goes before destruction, and a haughty spirit before a fall."

What is your course of action? God wants to save those we may deem un-redeemable. He wants us as His image bearers of light to go into the darkness and change the direction of action to reflect His principles. Are you willing to lay yourself down for this?

If yes, then you are ready to be an Actionvist.

I have shared with you my heart, my vulnerabilities, my pain & tragedy, my joy and my laughter. I have shared with you the steps I have taken to be where I am today as an overcomer. It has been hard and treacherous, but I would not change one thing because it has brought me to where I am.

I am going to conclude with one more piece for you to reflect on. Next page!

CONCLUSION TO REFLECT UPON

I HOLD THE STORY of Zacchaeus near and dear to my heart! It is my favorite story of the Bible. I encourage you to please take time to read Luke 19:1-10 ESV or TPT—my recommended translations.

Zacchaeus' name means purity, and he was what we would consider today to be a corrupt politician. He was the chief tax collector in his day.

The story of Zacchaeus begins with him hearing about this guy named Jesus. There was something deep within him that drove him to do an "about-face," and leave his business, status, and position behind.

Right then and there, Zacchaeus laid his life down. That's humility. Next you will note in the story that he is driven to get Jesus in his sight. Count how many times he tries to get a line of sight for Jesus. He also had the short man syndrome. He climbed up the sycamore tree (fig tree) in order that he could get a glimpse of Jesus. Zacchaeus' name meaning purity is not something to dismiss.

Also, it's important to note the sycamore tree.

In that day, if you were a gatherer of sycamore fruit like the Prophet Amos, you were there from the beginning through the end of the cultivation period to harvest.

See, if you or I were to take a bite of the sycamore fruit, it would be nearly impossible to eat for it is extremely bitter. Our mouths would fill up with the sour puss and wasps. So the gatherer of the fruit would have to pierce the fruit in order that the fruit would drain of the sour puss and the wasps, then ripen until it was ready to harvest to eat. Then, and only then, would you enjoy a sweet piece of fruit.

Zacchaeus was literally climbing that tree through humility (as he had left everything behind to get a glimpse of Jesus) and asking God to pierce him of everything in him that was sour and to drain him of anything holding him back from righteousness.

Jesus then immediately comes to the base of the tree and looks up to Zacchaeus (PURITY). "Come down for I am coming to dwell in your house today."

It says that Zacchaeus scurried down the tree and received Jesus joyfully.

Jesus never said, "You lousy scoundrel you. Look at what you have done!"

Instead, He spoke to him in the reflection that God saw him and sees us (purity). He called him higher because Zacchaeus had already laid his old life down. As a result of Zacchaeus' encounter with Jesus (RIGHTEOUSNESS), his heart was convicted. Not in shame or condemnation. He instantly repented and said he would give back anyone he cheated four times as much as he had stolen, and he would give half of what he owned to the poor.

While all of this was playing out, the crowd jeered, complained, ridiculed, and mocked both of them. However, they did not allow those individuals or what they said define their moment or their future. They stayed in a place of "rest" and kept in union with one another.

Jesus' response to Zacchaeus was this (TPT), "Your repentance shows that today life has come to you and your household, and that you are a true son of Abraham. The Son of Man has come to seek out and to give life to those who are lost. This is the picture and the perfect example of how we can move as statesmen (women) in this hour. Jesus sees you in the reflection as an overcomer. Not a victim.

The question remains, "Do you believe and trust in Him?"

Can you now believe you are an

overcomer? Actionvism!

Go forth and make the *numbers* of your days count starting now.

Numbers 6:24-26: "The Lord bless you and keep you; the Lord make his face shine on you and be gracious to you; the Lord turn his face toward you and give you peace."

Love to all!

~ *Lynz*

MY RECOMMENDED
RESOURCES AND READING

IT WAS ORIGINALLY my intention to define modern day slavery and different forms of trafficking. Instead, I have posted a link below in order that you can research the Department of Justice's definitions of such things.

The definition of freedom—in my mind—is the exchange Christ's blood in place of ours on the cross. Beaten, battered, and slashed, He exchanged our bondage with His blood. Bondage and slavery is defined as the exchange of someone or something for profit. Christ exchanged himself for us. You are FREE in Him.

It is time for the chains to break, the prison doors to open, bondage to collapse, and for slavery to end. It is time for hate and division to meet their demise. We must not spend our lifetimes defining who we are and our identity. We must rise up with an understanding of who—and whose—we are and spend our lifetime fulfilling the mandates and destiny of why God called us.

The Greatest and Best resource for you is the Living Word of God: the Bible. He has prepared the way for you and for me in order that we can prepare the way for Him here on Earth as it is in Heaven.

Modern Day Slavery As Sourced by the US Department of Justice:
https://www.state.gov/what-is-modern-slavery/

https://www.blueletterbible.org/

God bless you.

Made in the USA
Columbia, SC
21 October 2024

44785487R00117